PART

OF

ME

THE INNER TEAM DIALOGUE GUIDE

PART
OF
ME

Learn Who You Really Are, What's Driving You, and How to Get Out of Your Own Way

PAUL WYMAN

Cover design and layout by *the*BookDesigners,
https://bookdesigners.com/

First printing, 2024
Inner Team Dialogue
Longmont, Colorado, USA

www.innerteamdialogue.com

Paperback ISBN: 979-8-9905499-0-6
Ebook ISBN: 979-8-9905499-1-3

DEDICATION

To every part of you (yes, I mean all of them).

For Anne, who has not only patiently tolerated the
parts-geek in me, but has encouraged me at every step.

ACKNOWLEDGMENTS

I'm immensely grateful for the friendship and support of Ken Durbin, Lori Siegworth, Annie Boyum and Lindsay Fields-Goltz, who refused to allow me to talk myself out of embarking on this journey. You all believed in me and the importance of getting this work into the world, even when I was full of doubt.

I am indebted to the incredible coaches who now form the Inner Team Dialogue practitioner community. Your inexhaustible curiosity – about yourself, your clients and what's possible - has allowed ITD to expand and deepen beyond anything I could have conceived. Claire Williams was the spark, with her casual suggestion that I should teach this work. You ignited something in me.

The ideas in this book were influenced by the brilliant minds of dozens of coaches, including Julie Maloney, Beth Ronsick, Donna Zajonc, Lynn Pollard, Tamar Kagan, Victoria de Onis, Rachel Leone Marx, Kelly Dobson, Karen Hutchison, Tracy Burke, Brenda Goodwin, Karen Jacke, Sharon Ilstrup, Leslie Goldenberg, Jenny Peterson, Vera Shevchenko, Nikki Shultz, Rebecca Williams, Kristen Ell, Christy Vincent, Lynn Son Kee, Barrett Thompson, Kathy Lu,

Crista Jonson. Consultants Brad Todd, Yannick Nelson and Erica Breuer each provided essential insights at just the right moment.

A huge thank you to my brilliant writing coach and editor Cynthia Morris, for her unwavering support as I discovered my winding path to being an author. This book wouldn't exist without your clarity, flexibility and insight.

And most of all, to countless coaching clients who shared their characters with me over the past 25 years, and taught me how the Inner Team really works.

ITD stands on a foundation built by the beautiful work of Hal and Sidra Stone, the founders of Voice Dialogue, and the many teachers of this approach who've kept the flame burning. I'm indebted to Francesca Starr and Tamar Stone, whose brilliant teaching opened the door, and made this extraordinary body of work come alive for me almost 30 years ago.

WHO THIS BOOK IS FOR

Dear Reader:

If you picked up this book hoping for quick fixes or simple formulas to solve the immediate problems you're facing in your life, this is not the book for you. This book speaks to an aspiration for what your life can be which is larger than an absence of problems.

Part of Me is for seekers who aspire to live in a more wholehearted, conscious and compassionate way, who value the journey of personal development as much as its benefits.

That's not to say that this approach doesn't solve real problems. It does. Those who've set out on this journey have experienced:

- Greater self-confidence
- A significant decrease in self-criticism
- The capacity to make changes to long-standing habits of behavior
- Wiser decision making, with less second-guessing
- Enhanced intimacy and connectedness in relationships

But the larger intention behind this work is becoming a more whole, integrated you. In the words of Oprah Winfrey, "The whole point of being alive is to evolve into the complete person you were intended to be." Unconditional self-compassion is both how you achieve this expansion, and an outcome of the process.

Beyond the positive changes you may notice in yourself, the day-to-day experience of leading your Inner Team is inherently rewarding. It's a practice, in the way that yoga is a practice. Yoga can improve your strength and flexibility, but that's not why you keep showing up on your mat. It's because the experience of practicing is life-giving. It brings you into a closer relationship with who you are in the present moment.

Leading your Inner Team is similar. It's a practice that grows and deepens over time. It's not about <u>overcoming</u> the beliefs, feelings and habits of behavior that you've developed over the course of your life, or replacing them with better alternatives. It's about being compassionately present with them, accepting them and embracing them as part of what makes you, you.

You may not like certain tendencies you notice within yourself, such as people pleasing or habitual overthinking. You may even wish to get rid of the parts of you which are the source of these patterns. But when you can embrace these as lifelong companions rather than obstacles to be overcome, you'll notice a profound relaxation within. You will no longer go to war with yourself. The energy spent in self-judgment and suppressing parts of who you are will be liberated. It's gently expansive.

There's also an earthy humanness to this approach. There's no requirement to cultivate an elevated consciousness, only an invitation to observe and embrace the delightful, human mess of being you. As you start to relax into leading your Inner Team, you will likely find yourself to be more amused than critical of each character's predictable reactions. Inner Team Dialogue can be deep, tender and even sacred, and it can be surprising, hilarious, and downright absurd.

And the journey begins with an invitation: *your Inner Team needs a leader, and that leader is you.*

Paul Wyman
March 2024

CONTENTS

Part One: The Inner Team **1**

1. Introducing Multiple Mind 3
2. Characters in Teams 15
3. Principles of the Inner Team 35

Part Two: The Cast of Characters **45**

4. The Field Guide to the Inner Team 47
5. The Vulnerable Child 213
6. The Inner Critic 231

Part Three: Leading Your Inner Team **243**

7. The Inner Leader 245
8. Decision Making 257
9. Exercises, Reflections and Journaling Prompts 277
10. A Vision of Radical Inclusion 289

Afterword: How Writing a Book about the Inner Team
Taught Me How My Inner Team Really Works 293

Appendix **307**

Glossary of Terms 307
Origins of ITD 311
Continuing your Inner Team Journey 313

HOW TO GET THE MOST
FROM THIS BOOK

If you're not a cover-to-cover reader, here are some suggestions for how to get the most from this book.

Part I: The Inner Team dives deep into the idea of multiple mind, and how it departs from conventional views of the personality. If you're new to exploring parts, this is an essential foundation, because it helps you understand who you are in a completely new way.

Part II: The Cast of Characters features detailed profiles of fifty parts within. Almost all are presented in pairs of opposites (polarities). The Inner Critic and Vulnerable Child get chapters of their own, reflecting their importance to understanding your Inner Team.

Use the "diagnostic" chart at the beginning of chapter four to help you identify which pairs might be of greatest relevance to you. It's helpful to take notes about your experience of these parts.

Part III: Leading Your Inner Team

Once you've read about some of the characters and have identified which might be your Insiders and Outsiders, you're ready to begin exploring what it means to lead your Inner Team. Chapter 10 explores decision making in partnership with your Inner Team. Chapter 11 features a series of exercises to practice connecting with, learning from and ultimately learning to lead your characters.

PART 1
THE INNER TEAM

"Everybody has a secret world inside them. All the people of
the world, I mean everybody. No matter how dull and boring
they are on the outside, inside them they've all got unimag-
inable, magnificent, wonderful, stupid, amazing worlds. Not
just one world. Hundreds of them. Thousands maybe."

NEIL GAIMAN

CHAPTER 1

INTRODUCING MULTIPLE MIND

This chapter explores:

- *The multiple mind view of personality*
- *How multiple mind differs from a conventional monomind view*
- *The impact of monomind and multiple mind on how you grow*
- *How you can become aware of your multiple mind*

What if I told you that there's nothing wrong with you?

This is such a radical thought. We live in a society that for thousands of years has operated by the assumption that our true nature is flawed and sinful. Being a good person means ruthlessly suppressing and controlling your negative impulses.

When you believe that some parts of your personality are bad, you turn yourself into a problem to be solved.

But it doesn't have to be this way. You do not need to be "fixed". A small shift in who you think you are changes everything.

It's the shift from thinking that you have a single personality with good and bad traits, to recognizing that your personality is multiple, plural, and diverse. Whether you call them parts, sub-personalities, selves, or characters, the principle on which the Inner Team rests is that every part is trying to protect you. None are trying to sabotage you. No part wants you to suffer.

As you release the impulse to pass judgment on the parts you observe within yourself, deep compassion begins to emerge in its place. Where you once would have cringed in shame about a part of yourself you considered "bad", you'll discover the capacity to respond to it with curiosity and humor.

But how do you know your personality is multiple?

NOTICING YOUR MULTIPLICITY

Multiple mind isn't just a theory, it's how you experience yourself every day.

How many of these nine common indicators of multiplicity have you noticed in yourself?

1. Do you use parts language when talking about yourself?
Phrases like, "A part of me wants..." or "I'm in two minds about..." directly name what it feels like to experience your multiplicity as distinct drives and impulses within.

2. Do you experience ambivalence?
Ambivalence is the feeling of being pulled in two directions at once. It's produced by the tension between two parts of you that have different desires and goals. For example, part of you wants to tell your boss what you really think, and another part of you tells you to play it safe and keep your big mouth shut.

3. Do you experience mixed feelings?

Your capacity to experience multiple, contradictory emotions at the same time points to the presence of different parts within you, each reacting differently to the same stimulus. For example, you love your sibling, but you don't want them to come to stay. You feel grateful to have a stable job, but you also feel trapped. Our language is peppered with terms for mixed feelings, such as "bittersweet", the experience of feeling both sad and happy at the same time.

4. Do you argue with yourself?

When you face an important choice, does it feel like there's a debate going on inside you? Parts want to guide your behavior, and will whisper (or yell!) their concerns and counter-arguments, until you're thoroughly confused about which way to turn. Much of your thinking is best understood as conversations between different parts of your personality.

5. Do you feel like a different person in certain situations, or with certain people?

You don't show up the same way in every context or every relationship, because different parts of your personality come forward in different roles and relationships in your life. Perhaps you're intense and driven at work, laid back at home. Perhaps you're more serious with your brother, more playful with your sister. Which is the real you? Both!

6. Do you sometimes behave out of character, in a way that makes little sense to you?

Perhaps you're in a committed, monogamous relationship, but

you become uncharacteristically flirty at a party. Or you come home from the store with an impulse buy, despite being a financially cautious person. When your behavior deviates from your established patterns in unexpected ways, your underused or forgotten parts are temporarily taking the wheel.

7. Are you attracted to your opposite?

You're emotional, he's coolly rational. You're serious and responsible, he's playful and carefree. When you're with this person, they unlock a part of who you are which you'd normally find d to access, and it's *irresistible*. When you don't have connection with a part within yourself, you'll discover it in other people, and it feels a bit like a crush. It's best understood as an attempt to reconnect with a part of who you are, to become more whole.

8. Are you repelled from your opposite?

Paradoxically, the same qualities that can magnetically draw you to other people can also be repellent. When you have a disproportionately negative reaction to someone, they may represent a part of yourself you see negatively. For example, you might find that you can't stand that coolly rational guy, seeing him as cold and unfeeling. You might judge the playful guy, seeing him as dangerously irresponsible. It's your own rational and playful parts that you're judging, and projecting onto the other person.

9. You don't quite fit any personality "type"

Many personality typologies, from Myers-Briggs to the Enneagram, propose that you have a single personality "type." While you may indeed have many of the characteristics associated with your "type," you have probably noticed that you also demonstrate several of the attitudes, traits and behaviors associated with the other types. This is because your type describes only the parts of your personality you're most identified with, not its entirety. Every type is within you.

MULTIPLE MIND IS NOT A PATHOLOGY

The experience of oneself as multiple is quite normal. There's nothing pathological about having mixed feelings, out-of-character impulses or arguments with yourself.

Unfortunately, multiplicity has been pathologized, associated with serious mental illnesses like Dissociative Identity Disorder (previously called Multiple Personality Disorder). Dissociative Identity Disorder is an extreme form of multiplicity, the product of trauma severe enough to fragment the mind. In DID, subpersonalities become "alters" with no awareness of other parts. In the absence of this kind of shattering trauma, however, your subpersonalities do not take over your behavior, nor cause you to act without volition.

The association between multiplicity and mental illness can be traced back to movies like *Sybil* (1973) and *The Many Faces of Eve* (1957). Books like Dr Jekyll and Mr. Hyde have perpetuated the same mythologies about parts taking over behavior. While these make for dramatic stories, their unintended impact has been to generate fear of what is a perfectly ordinary experience.

When you look to sources more reliable than Hollywood, there are many psychological systems which operate from a multiple mind view of personality. Internal Family Systems is perhaps the best known at present. Others include Psychosynthesis,

Schema Therapy, Voice Dialogue, Gestalt and Transactional Analysis. Inner Team Dialogue, the approach described in this book, is a branch of that same tree.

Once you move beyond the fear of multiplicity, multiple mind offers you not just a more nuanced understanding of your personality, but also a radically different and gentler path towards growth.

THE MONOMIND VIEW OF PERSONALITY

Multiple mind isn't a new concept, but it is a long way from being the conventional view of personality. The dominant view still sees personality as singular. Richard Schwartz, Ph.D., founder of Internal Family Systems, has termed the default view of personality "monomind".

What follows is a summary of the Monomind view of personality, and its implications for your relationship with yourself, and your path of inner development. *As you read, notice which of these assumptions and beliefs sound familiar.*

Because you have one brain, you believe you also have one mind, which is the source of all your feelings, thoughts, impulses and behavior.

Some of your thoughts and impulses are good, some are bad. If you have bad thoughts, it follows that you must be bad too.

In your effort to be good, you try to suppress or deny those bad thoughts with willpower, or correct them with more positive thoughts, or attempt to pray or meditate them away. You strive to live from your "higher" self, and suppress your lower, more selfish instincts.

You are now at war with yourself, fighting against your badness. Your Inner Critic leads the charge in this battle, using fierce criticism to shame you into behaving "right", and labeling you a worthless failure if you don't.

But your effort to suppress or transcend your negative thoughts with willpower doesn't work very well. You try to replace negative with positive thoughts, but your negative thoughts don't go away. They keep rising to the surface.

Each time you think a negative thought, your Inner Critic piles on, berating you for your terrible personality which is full of shameful, sinful impulses that you have consistently failed to control.

Your lack of self-control and weak self-discipline compound the problem of your flawed personality. You work hard to keep your "true" nature hidden, by carefully curating the persona you show the world. You reason that if people saw the real you, you'd be rejected, your unworthiness laid bare.

In search of greater control, you dabble with personal growth and spiritual development approaches, each of which promises to help you be better than the unworthy wretch you fear that you truly are. Some even promise that not only will you fix your flaws, but you will also discover your "higher" self.

Sound familiar?

You'll find this monomind view of personality everywhere you look. Anywhere you see exhortations to use willpower, grit or self-discipline to achieve personal change, this monomind belief is in charge. The belief that you have to criticize, judge and shame yourself into change, also arises from monomind assumptions.

Using shame and self-criticism to motivate yourself to "fix" your bad traits is the source of so much suffering. But it doesn't have to be this way.

THE MULTIPLE MIND VIEW OF PERSONALITY

Multiple mind offers a completely different – and far more compassionate – approach to understanding who you are, and how you develop. *As you read, notice which of these assumptions and beliefs sound familiar.*

You notice your thoughts and your impulses, but decide not to pass judgment on whether they are good or bad. Instead, you get curious about them.

What's immediately evident is that you're not consistent. Some days, your thinking is optimistic, other days pessimistic. Sometimes you're skeptical, sometimes you're trusting.

You wonder "Which is the real me?", but decide this isn't a very useful question, because they all seem to be the real you. You're optimistic <u>and</u> pessimistic, skeptical <u>and</u> trusting.

You wonder whether optimism is better than pessimism, or skepticism is better than being trusting. Both seem useful at different times.

You don't feel the need to judge one as better than the other, any more than you need to choose whether you prefer your right or left leg.

You conclude that your personality must have many parts to produce such contrasting patterns of thought. You imagine each part of your personality to be like a whole person inside you, each with its own worldview, beliefs and approach to life. Each part has strong opinions about how you should stay safe, earn love and avoid pain.

The more you pay attention to these parts within you, the more you recognize your thinking as debates between parts, each trying to persuade you towards their preferred path to safety.

You recognize that all these paths seem coherent, possessing their own wisdom.

With a sigh of relaxation, you settle into the knowledge that no part of you is bad. Even parts that push you to behave in ways that don't seem very effective are trying, in the only ways they know how, to protect you.

You wonder how it is that you can be aware of these parts. As you observe what's going on inside you, the realization comes to you that you are not your parts, you are their observer. As you learn to witness and listen to each with compassion, you realize that you are not only observing, but can exercise choice about how you use these parts in your everyday life.

EMBRACING MULTIPLICITY

Multiple mind holds that the normal state of being human isn't coherence and consistency, but contradiction, ambivalence and inner conflict between parts. Only the belief that we <u>should</u> only feel or think one thing at a time turns this experience into a problem.

You may notice the impulse to judge the parts within you as good or bad, or take sides between them. While this seems like a pathway to knowing your own mind, a way to achieve a kind of inner clarity and certainty, the opposite happens. When you choose to privilege one part of you and silence another, you actually know your own mind <u>less</u> well. You're paying attention to only a part of who you are.

Rather than trying to "resolve" your internal contradictions, it's possible to embrace and even celebrate them. Psychologist

John Rowan (in <u>Discover Your Subpersonalities</u>, 1993) offers a beautiful metaphor to capture this relationship to our multiplicity:

> "Sometimes the sky is blue, sometimes shaded by clouds or roaring with thunder. Sometimes it's dark as the night and sometimes red as fire. Still we see it as one sky and not a fragmented sky or a sky with multiple-color-disorder.
>
> To me, the self is a process, not an object. It is like taking pictures of a river during different seasons and arguing "Which is the authentic self of the river?"
>
> Or "How many selves does the river have?" If we define the river as the picture, then the answer is "as many pictures you take!"

When you set aside your judgments of good and bad, and turn towards the mixed feelings and contradictory impulses within you, it opens up a completely different kind of experience of yourself.

In place of the shame you may have felt about what you've labeled "negative" thoughts or impulses, it's possible to cultivate curiosity. When you turn towards these parts, you'll discover that all of them (really, <u>all</u> of them) are trying to protect you, to guide you towards what they believe is the best way for you to be safe in the world. The parts deserve your gratitude more than your judgment.

With this gratitude and curiosity, what emerges is that there's more to you than you once thought. There's the person you were raised to be. The person you had to become to survive the dangers of your early environment. The person your partner needs you to be. The person your boss needs you to be.

And there's also the person you forgot you could be, the person you weren't allowed to be, the person you swore you'd never become.

They're all you.

Exploring your multiplicity is a journey of getting reacquainted with <u>all</u> these parts of who you are, remembering how they came to be, celebrating all that they have done for you. It's a journey of re-admitting the parts of you that weren't safe to embrace years ago.

This makes it possible to set aside limited definitions of who you are, such as a single personality type or a role, in order to embrace a fuller, more complete version of yourself, a beautifully messy, complex, contradictory human being.

Portuguese poet Fernando Pessoa captured this perfectly: "In every corner of my soul there is an altar to a different god."

CHAPTER 2

CHARACTERS IN TEAMS

This chapter explores:

- *What are characters (aka parts, selves or subpersonalities)?*
- *The metaphor of the Inner Team*
- *The Inner Leader*
- *Insiders and Outsiders*

Psychologist Carl Jung wrote in 1946, "A man who seems to be one is not one, but as many different persons appear in him as he has attitudes."

But what are these "persons within"? Or perhaps more usefully, *who* are they? Where do they come from? How do they operate within you?

These "persons within" that Jung describes have had many names, including *subpersonalities, parts, selves* and *voices*. In Inner Team Dialogue, we call them *Characters*, because we experience them as having distinct personalities of their own. There are times when it can feel like you've been temporarily taken over by a part of who you are which has its own style, language, beliefs, attitudes, even its own body posture.

You do not, of course, have tiny people running around inside your skull. So what is a character, exactly?

THE DEFINITION OF A CHARACTER

A character is *a consistent and identifiable pattern of thoughts, feelings, sensations and beliefs, manifesting as a set of rules for behavior.*

Characters are more than temporary emotional states or passing thoughts. Their patterns of thought and behavior show up consistently, and seem to operate with enough autonomy that they feel like whole people with an agenda of their own. We experience their presence as a repeating thought in the mind, a familiar feeling in the heart, a sensation in the body, and a familiar belief about the way things are.

Consistent Thoughts: We're not talking about passing thoughts here, but repeating ones. During a presentation at work, perhaps you think, "Wow, this is taking a long time!" This is not necessarily a sign that a character is the source of that thought. If, however, that thought comes up repeatedly, perhaps when you're helping your daughter get dressed for school, and when you're sitting in traffic, and when you're waiting for a call back from a colleague, then it's highly likely that you're hearing from a character within you who thinks that things should move fast.

The more frequently you think the same thought, the more

likely it is to come from a character. If you have the same conversation with yourself over and over again, one of your characters is steering your thinking down a well-trodden mental path.

Consistent Feelings: If there's a particular emotional state you feel regularly, in multiple situations, that can also indicate the presence of one of your characters. For example, does anger surge quickly in you, with only minimal provocation? Do minor disappointments consistently drop you into the same deep pool of sadness? Do you meet new people with a familiar fluttering of excitement and hope, or anxiety that they're going to judge you and find you wanting? When your emotional reactions follow consistent patterns, rather than being fleeting sensations, you're experiencing the emotional state of one of the characters.

Consistent Sensations: Consider sensations you experience frequently in your body, which accompany familiar mental and emotional states. For example, do you experience a headache when you're pushing yourself to complete a long task list? A knot in your stomach when you're about to speak in a group? These are the somatic indicators of a character on your Inner Team being activated.

Imagine the different body posture of a part of you that is confident and assertive, compared to a part of you that's full of self-doubt. Standing tall or with shoulders hunched may be more than postural habits. They may indicate which characters are exerting their influence on how you inhabit your body.

Beliefs: What do you know *for sure* about how the world works? That every accomplishment requires hard work and struggle? That your worth depends on how others see you? That people in

17

authority cannot be trusted?

Among all the beliefs that you carry, some feel like capital-T Truths. They reflect a way of making meaning, a consistent interpretation of what we see, hear and feel. The characters within us are the carriers of these stable beliefs.

Rules of Behavior

These beliefs become the rationale for our behaviors. If you believe that people are trustworthy, behaviors like self-disclosure and transparency naturally express this belief. If you believe that people cannot be trusted, behaviors like guardedness and withholding are justified and reasonable.

These rules of behavior guide our actions automatically, without conscious awareness. They are our "autopilot" settings, our most habitual ways of being in the world.

Here's an example of how thoughts, feelings, sensations and beliefs produce a consistent set of rules of behavior that come together to form a character called the Perfectionist:

*The **thought** that my writing isn't clear enough generates a **feeling** of anxiety, which is accompanied by a **sensation** of tension in my shoulders. I have a **belief** that I won't be understood unless my writing is perfect. When I sit down to write, I follow a **rule of behavior** that says every sentence must be perfect, so I edit and re-write endlessly, and rarely finish anything.*

CHARACTERS MAKE THEIR PRESENCE KNOWN IN DIFFERENT WAYS

Characters such as Rational or Observer produce a lot of mental activity, so you may notice them primarily as thoughts or internal conversations. Feeling and Playful, by contrast, are more likely to come into your awareness through specific emotions or moods. Pusher and Thrill Seeker bring such a high level of energy that you may notice them most readily as distinctive body sensations.

No matter how they get your attention, all characters have rules of behavior, which tell you what you should or shouldn't do to be safe. For this reason, your "shoulds" and "shouldn'ts" are the most consistent way of identifying a character.

WHERE DO CHARACTERS COME FROM?

Characters are best understood as **personifications of schemas**. A schema is a map of how the world works which you create based on your experience. Schemas are predictions of what's about to happen, based on what has happened before. They operate below the level of your awareness, helping you instantly access successful behaviors without the need to consciously decide what to do.

Your schemas hold your deepest learnings about the world, including what's safe to express and what should stay hidden; how to relate to others; what behaviors win love, approval and inclusion, and what behaviors expose you to judgment, exclusion or rejection.

Schemas can form as a response to a repeated experience, such as being consistently rewarded or punished for a behavior.

They can also form as a response to a single, intense experience. The more powerful the emotions when the schema was formed – from trauma, or any experience with heightened emotional intensity – the more persistent they become, and the more resistant to change, because you associate them with survival.

THE INNER TEAM METAPHOR

Individual characters can be identified through their consistent thoughts, feelings, behaviors and beliefs, but none operates alone. A simple metaphor of an Inner Team helps illuminate how characters work together to create the near-universal experience of a "committee in your head".

Imagine that all the characters within you were members of a team. The team has a single objective: to make sure you stay safe and avoid pain.

Picture a dozen members of this team sitting around a conference table, having a discussion. Three of them do most of the talking, dominating the conversation about what you should and shouldn't do to stay safe. A couple of others occasionally offer a suggestion. The remainder stay largely silent. There are a few names on the team roster who don't appear to have been invited to the meeting at all.

As you listen to the three main contributors, you notice how certain they sound. They exude total confidence that their solutions to keep you safe will work. They're not shy about asserting their opinions. They have specific examples to back up their positions. They are quick to tell you what terrible things will happen if you don't follow their advice.

On the rare occasions that their opinions are challenged, they push back, hard. They offer a forceful rebuttal, spiced with a disparaging comment or two about their challenger.

The team is quite diverse, but only a few are actively contributing. You wonder what the silent members are thinking.

It occurs to you that the team really needs a leader who can draw them out, and make it safe to dissent, challenge and debate.

THE LEADER OF THE INNER TEAM

The most important element of this metaphor is neither the members of the team, nor how they interact. It's who is doing the noticing.

If you were to tell me, "I have a Perfectionist on my Inner Team", who's the "I" in that sentence? There is a you, which is separate from the characters within. We call this observing presence the Inner Leader.

The Inner Leader's role is to understand the team's members, and their patterns of interaction. It's the Inner Leader who notices the characters who are over-contributing or remaining silent. But the Inner Leader is far from a passive observer: over time, the Inner Leader takes on a more and more active role in managing the contribution of all the members of the team.

All of the insights of this system, and all of the benefits it can offer in your development, come from cultivating the Inner Leader. A more in-depth exploration of the Inner Leader can be found in chapter nine.

A LEADERSHIP VACUUM ON THE INNER TEAM

One of the simplest ways to understand the Inner Leader's importance is to consider what happens to a team that has no leader.

A team without a leader has a leadership vacuum. And because nature abhors a vacuum, the most confident and assertive members of your Inner Team will rush in to fill it.

Without a leader to interrupt their patterns, these dominant characters will dictate your thoughts, feelings, reactions and behaviors. They will guide your behavior towards what they perceive to be good, safe and right, and away from behaviors they consider bad, dangerous or wrong. The Inner Critic will operate as an enforcer of these rules.

When your life is controlled by these dominant parts, you will have an effective but narrow set of solutions to the challenges you face. For example, if your Inner Team is being run by a "Pusher" part, you will attempt to solve all your problems through hard work. If it's being run by a "Rational" part, you will attempt to solve all your problems by study, analysis and rational deduction. You'll have all the strengths associated with these approaches, but you'll lack alternatives to draw upon when hard work or rationality are the wrong tools for the job.

This is the default condition for most people, until the Inner Leader takes over, and can engage the capabilities of the rest of the team.

Insiders

The characters who play a dominant role on your Inner Team are called **Insiders**. Think of them as the "in-crowd" of your Inner Team. They're the power players and the loudest voices. Your Insiders are your identity, your persona, who you think you are. Most people can identify three to five Insiders, but there's no upper limit.

Insiders describe your most reliable, well-practiced strategies to deal with the challenges in your life. They are the source of your superpowers and major contributors to your successes. They represent what you do automatically, reflexively, without requiring a conscious decision. They're so familiar that you wouldn't recognize yourself if you weren't following their rules.

Your Insiders are <u>fiercely</u> protective of you. Each believes that its strategy to protect you is so critical to your survival that it must be maintained at all costs. Insiders resist any attempt to minimize or decrease their influence. They have power on your Inner Team, and they're not about to let go of it. They maintain their power by actively warning you against the dangers of listening to other characters (Outsiders) who hold a different perspective.

Hidden Insiders
All Insiders exert a powerful influence on your thought patterns and behaviors, but **hidden Insiders** do this from behind the scenes. An Insider is considered hidden if you do not consciously acknowledge its presence or influence, but it nevertheless prompts consistent reactions or impulses in you.

When hidden Insiders directly impact your behavior, they produce a particular kind of confusion about yourself *("I don't know why I keep doing that.")*

A common example of a hidden Insider is the Indulger. You consciously try to eat healthily, but you find yourself on the couch next to an empty box of Oreos, wondering how that happened. The indulgent part of you, which wants pleasure right now, directed your behavior, even as you identify with the part of you which is focused on your long-term health (the Restrictor).

A hidden Insider that operates in many people is the Patriarch. You may bristle at the suggestion that your Inner Team includes a character who believes men are superior to women. But it's the Patriarch who whispers in your ear that women need to be as tough as men to make it in the workplace, or generates a negative first impression of a powerful woman.

A character like the Patriarch can be a hidden Insider even if you never act on its promptings. Hidden Insiders most commonly show up as a set of unconscious assumptions, which drive our thinking and behavior.

IDENTIFYING YOUR INSIDERS

A quick way to understand who your Insiders might be is to think of a single adjective that describes your personality. The adjective you choose will point unerringly at one of your Insiders.

Example Insider Adjectives[1]

COMMON ADJECTIVE	INSIDER CHARACTER
Creative	Artist
Practical	Pragmatist
Flexible	Chameleon
Consistent	Zebra
Adventurous	Thrill Seeker
Team-Player	Collaborator

1 Note: some characters which are featured in the field guide are not included on this list, because their adjective is identical to their name, such as Competitor, Loyalist or Indulger.

Confident	Expert
Curious	Learner
Controlling	Controller
Permissive	Allower
Independent	Independent
Receiver	Dependent
Indulgent	Indulger
Disciplined	Restrictor
Discerning	Judge
Concrete	Material
Inspired	Spiritual
Dramatic	Maximizer
Unique	Special
Precise	Perfectionist
Random	Messy
Organized	Planner
Spontaneous	Improviser
Kind	Pleaser
Firm	Boundaried
Cautious	Protector
Productive	Pusher
Present	Being
Logical	Rational
Sensitive	Feeling
Committed	Responsible
Fun loving	Playful
Obedient	Rule Follower
Oppositional	Rebel
Direct	Warrior
Calm	Peacemaker

THE OPERATING COMMITTEE

This term describes a tight-knit group of Insider characters who cooperate, support and reinforce each other. The Operating Committee is largely indistinguishable from what you describe as your personality.

For example, a team of Perfectionist, Pusher and Pleaser is a common Operating Committee. The Perfectionist sets the standards for quality, the Pusher drives you to put in the hard work to achieve those standards, and the Pleaser makes sure the work meets the needs and expectations of others.

These are the same characters who guard against their opposites (Messy, Being and Boundaried), making sure you are aware only of the downsides of these characters, in this case warning you against deadly sins of making mistakes, resting, or disappointing others.

There are an infinite number of combinations of characters who form an operating committee. Yours might be less conventional, such as a combination of Artist, Rebel and Spiritual. It might be a powerhouse combination like Pusher, Competitor and Warrior.

Whatever the combination of characters, your Operating Committee represents your default ways of showing up in the world, the behaviors you most consistently demonstrate. It's your autopilot setting.

OUTSIDERS

If your Insiders are who you think you are, your Outsiders are who you think you are not.

Outsiders are the parts of you who have been ignored, rejected, marginalized or even forgotten. They're the voices on your Inner Team that have been shouted down, silenced or suppressed.

It is your Insiders who turn characters into Outsiders. All Outsiders represent ways of thinking or behaving that directly clash with one or more of your Insiders, who will be quick to point out how the Outsider's behaviors are dangerous, risky, inappropriate or even shameful.

For example, the action-oriented, urgency-driven Pusher Insider clashes with its reflective, laid-back, patient opposite, Being. Pusher believes safety comes from getting as many tasks done as fast as possible, so pausing to reflect or (God forbid!) taking a nap when you're tired, breaks these rules of behavior.

The Insider sees the Outsider's qualities not as complementary strengths, but as threats to your survival. Insiders often attach negative labels to Outsiders to discourage you from even considering going there (characterizing Being as lazy, slow or complacent).

Outsider characters are part of every Inner Team, but they're always harder to see than your Insiders. Because they have been consistently judged and marginalized, many Outsiders go silent. Where your Insiders tend to be quick to offer you (often unsolicited!) advice, Outsiders tend to be reticent. This reticence is a natural reaction to how they have been treated: imagine how willing you'd be to share an idea in a meeting where you'd been repeatedly shouted down, or called mean names?

It's common to deny the presence of Outsiders within you altogether, and even more so to attempt to hide these parts of yourself from others. You might well feel offended if someone were to describe you in a way that indicates the presence of your Outsider. Think of a term you might find insulting: like being called lazy, selfish, or irresponsible. This reaction indicates that the part of you that is capable of being this way is something you have judged as bad. The strength of your negative reaction to this label directly correlates with the degree to which you have exiled this part, and judged it as bad, even shameful.

While Outsiders are inherently hard to see in yourself, they're easy to see in other people. For example, if you're identified with being hard working (Pusher Insider), you may have a hard time acknowledging and accepting the part of you that would rather lay on the couch and daydream (Being Outsider). But you might well see Being's quality in other people, and judge those people as lazy. One of the most direct ways to identify your Outsiders is to notice what irritates you most in other people. As the saying goes, if you spot it, you got it.

There are different degrees of Outsider, on a continuum from underused to completely forgotten.

Underused Outsiders

An underused Outsider is a character whom you call upon infrequently, even in situations where their strengths could be helpful.

For example, if your Insider is Rational, you may underuse its opposite, the emotionally attuned Feeling character, preferring to stay in your comfort zone of cool, objective thinking.

Underused Outsiders do not particularly threaten the Insiders, so you may not feel much conscious resistance to integrating them into your Inner Team. You may even desire more access to them. But they're unpracticed and often clumsy. To continue the Rational example, you may be very open to embracing your feeling side, recognizing the value of being emotionally intelligent. But from lack of practice, your Feeling character may be undeveloped, and it may be difficult to tune into exactly what you're really feeling, what your heart most desires, or what your intuition is telling you.

Situational Outsiders

Some underuse patterns are specific to a particular context. For example, many businesses celebrate (and promote) employees who embody Pusher, Responsible and Rational, and don't know quite what to do with those who embody Being, Playful and Feeling. So the latter three might become **situational outsiders**, which you suppress when you're at work, but would be completely comfortable expressing at home, or with your friends.

Everyone curates which parts of themselves they show in a particular context: it's inevitable, and probably necessary. But there is a cost. When you have to shut down a part of who you are to fit in, what's lost is true belonging, the feeling that you're truly valued and welcomed. And the effort that goes into suppressing these parts of yourself and keeping them hidden at work is considerable, and can be exhausting, contributing over time to professional burnout.

Consistent Outsiders

Some characters are <u>always</u> Outsiders in your Inner Team, representing parts of you that you (or, more accurately, your Insiders) have judged as bad, dangerous or inappropriate in <u>every</u> setting.

Characters who are judged as negative by society at large, such as Dependent or Being, are far more likely to become Outsiders than Insiders.

More commonly, however, Outsiders have a history that goes beyond a particular workplace or relationship. Characters which become Insiders are usually those whose expression would have exposed you to danger early in your life. For example, your mystically inclined spiritual character might have exposed you to judgment or humiliation in a secular family, and become an Outsider.

Forgotten Outsiders

This is the most extreme form of Outsider. These are the parts of yourself you cannot see, that you completely deny are within you. Your forgotten Outsiders are what you are 100% certain you're not. You deny them to yourself, and you hide them from others.

What's true of Outsiders throughout this continuum is that they are still within you, waiting for you to recognize them, see their gifts, and include them. They feel like what you're not, but it would be more accurate to say that they are what you have forgotten you are. Their re-integration into your Inner Team is not only profoundly healing, it also provides your Inner Team with resources that are of immense value. They might just hold the solutions to some of your most consistent challenges.

INNER TEAM DIALOGUE CASE STUDY:
Insiders and Outsiders

Soon after her promotion to an account lead role in her design agency, Vanessa made a presentation to a major client, who showered her with praise for the originality of the new designs. Vanessa deflected the praise, offering a self-deprecating deflection that the designs weren't really that original. An awkward silence followed.

One of her colleagues pulled her aside after the meeting, angry that Vanessa had talked down their work. The client had loved it, after all. If Vanessa didn't think it was original, why hadn't she said something before the meeting?

Vanessa was not only devastated by the feedback, she was also very confused about her own behavior. She was genuinely proud of her team's work, and delighted by the client's positive reaction. But her behavior had communicated exactly the opposite, and she didn't understand why.

As we reflected on this incident in her next coaching session, Vanessa shared that the moment the client paid her the compliment, she had experienced both a surge of pride, and a simultaneous, overwhelming impulse to run and hide, to be anywhere but in the spotlight. How was it possible that she could have two completely opposite responses at the same time?

I invited Vanessa to consider the possibility that one part of her loved attention, while another part of her was terrified by it. She agreed, and indicated an eagerness to explore both parts.

First, we spent some time getting to know the part of her that found attention excruciatingly vulnerable. This character, known as Ordinary, demanded that Vanessa always act with humility, and never draw attention to herself. Ordinary had become an Insider on Vanessa's Inner Team as a pre-teen after witnessing her older sister get shamed by her stepmother for dressing in a way that would draw attention to herself. Her stepmother's words, "Who do you think you are!" still made Vanessa's stomach churn with discomfort. She had made a decision there and then that the best way to stay safe was to become invisible.

Vanessa now had insight into which part of her had deflected the praise and produced the impulse to run and hide. If she was going to succeed in her new job, however, she had to find a way to cultivate the part of her that enjoyed receiving attention. This felt completely out of reach.

I suggested that the change she wanted to achieve would involve getting to know Ordinary's opposite, Special. But Vanessa had ruthlessly suppressed this character, exiling it from her Inner Team. She had been so successful at this that not only did she deny that Special was a part of her, she saw it exclusively as a negative trait. In her mind, specialness equaled arrogance, entitlement and elitism. Why on earth would she want to be more like that?

With a little encouragement that there might be more to Special than she was currently seeing, Vanessa began the work of re-establishing awareness of her Special part. She was surprised to discover that it wasn't some kind of attention hog who thought it was above the rules. It was the part of her that wanted to shine, to make its own unique contribution, to be seen as precious.

Vanessa's breakthrough was the moment she realized that Special had been operating within her all along. Her Special character was the source of her remarkable design sense, the very quality that got her promoted in the first place. She'd always had an unerring instinct for what imagery matched a brand, and what rang a false note.

Once Vanessa could find Special within her and see it as a positive influence, it changed everything. No longer was she trying to become something she was not, she was simply learning to apply Special's gifts to herself rather than to brand imagery. She set about trying to understand what made her distinctive, unique and precious. Even asking this question would have been a kind of heresy before she discovered Special as a member of her Inner Team.

Over time, she made progress. Her first reaction to anything that sounded like praise was still to deflect and minimize, but

Vanessa learned to pause this response, and stay present long enough to take it in. She decided to enlist friends to help her get more comfortable when receiving a compliment, a practice she called "micro-dosing" praise. It involved asking trusted colleagues at work to share what they appreciated about Vanessa's work. With each "dose" of praise, she would register the familiar squirming discomfort, reassure herself that she was safe, and let the compliment sink in. Not only did the intensity of her urge to escape the praise become less intense over time, she found - to her great surprise - that she began to rather enjoy it.

CHAPTER 3

PRINCIPLES OF THE INNER TEAM

This chapter explores the principles which govern how the Inner Team operates:

1. *No bad characters*
2. *Characters can only be themselves*
3. *Characters have opposites*
4. *Characters react like real people*
5. *Characters team up and work cooperatively*
6. *All characters protect the vulnerable child*

---

1. THERE ARE NO BAD CHARACTERS

This phrase, borrowing language from Dick Schwartz's book "No Bad Parts", captures the single most important principle in parts work. The Inner Team Dialogue approach operates from this premise.

Every character on your Inner Team is trying to protect you, in the only ways it knows how. Even those you have judged as negative, dangerous or even sinful have no agenda other than to protect you.

That's not to say characters can't cause problems for you: they can and they do. If you've ever been run ragged by your Pusher's relentless focus on completing tasks, or your Pleaser's compulsive need to take care of other people, you know the kind of problems your Inner Team characters can cause.

But this does not reflect something negative about the character itself. The problems they cause are not expressions of inherent badness, only that they are being overused, used at the wrong moment, used unskillfully, or used out of balance with their opposite.

This can be a hard idea to swallow, when you're experiencing a particularly vicious Inner Critic attack or your Perfectionist is pointing out all the flaws in your work.

The next time you start to wonder whether one of your characters is following a nefarious plan to undermine you, pause to consider the source of that thought. The perception that one of your characters is fundamentally bad always originates with another character, not the Inner Leader.

Characters judge each other as negative when they don't follow the rules of behavior which are there to keep you safe. For example, my Pusher is quite certain that its opposite, Being, is irredeemably bad, because it doesn't follow the rule of always working hard. What prompts the Pusher's judgment of its opposite is that Being breaks one of its most sacrosanct rules for how to stay safe.

Consider a negative label you've given yourself. Perhaps you've called yourself "selfish" when you prioritize your own needs over other people's. In this case, Pleaser is the character who is most likely to demand that you always put other people's needs before your own. It labels behavior arising from its opposite (Boundaried) as "selfish".

The Inner Leader, by contrast, sees every character as having a valuable point of view, and will listen openly to each. In the Pleaser example, it will see the value of both self-care and care for others.

To label a character a "saboteur," is both distorting and unhelpful, and a misapprehension of how characters work. It's certainly true that some characters on your Inner Team can oppose or resist what you are consciously aspiring to achieve in your life, and it's tempting to think of this as sabotage. But they resist because they are convinced that what you're doing is dangerous to your safety.

2. CHARACTERS CAN ONLY BE THEMSELVES

Pleasers please, Critics criticize, Pushers push. They cannot be otherwise.

Your Inner Critic won't suddenly have a breakthrough in awareness, see the error of its ways, and become your greatest cheerleader. The Inner Critic uses criticism to keep you safe, and it's not going to stop, because it believes to do so is to expose you to risks it's obligated to warn you about.

To say it another way, every character is a one-trick pony. Each holds a single, fixed point of view. They propose a single solution.

The Inner Leader's task isn't to get your characters to change what they do. It's to deploy the character's singular gifts when they can be of greatest service, and relieve them of sole responsibility for guarding your safety.

Since characters don't fundamentally change, change comes from you, the Inner Leader, deciding when to act upon the promptings of each character.

The only change you'll see from a character is a gradual increase in trust in you, the Inner Leader. As the character recognizes that you are taking ownership of its objective (achieving safety), it will be more willing to take a step back.

3. CHARACTERS HAVE OPPOSITES

Each character on the Inner Team has one or more opposites which play a complementary, balancing role.

For example, the part of you that wants to fit in is balanced by a part of you that wants to stand out. The part of you which navigates the world by reason is balanced by the part which is guided by passion.

These opposites are inescapable tensions that everyone must wrestle with, to a greater or lesser degree. The technical term for how these opposite forces relate to each other is a polarity. This concept draws on the work of Barry Johnson, who defines a Polarity as "a pair of opposite, seemingly contradictory states which are interdependent."

Polarities are inherently unsolvable. They are balances to find, not problems to solve. Choosing one side of a polarity over another is a bit like choosing whether you prefer your left or right leg. Walking is considerably easier when you use both.

Balancing polarities requires a shift in thinking from either/or to both/and. But finding this both/and balance between opposites can be challenging.

When one character is an Insider on your Inner Team, it increases the chances that its opposite will be an Outsider. We have preferences for one side of most polarities, in the same sense that we have a dominant and non-dominant hand.

You can think of opposites as being like enemies or antagonists in a drama. Each views the other skeptically, if not openly critically. Because your Insiders are charged with keeping you safe, they see their opposites as threats to that safety. For example, a Pusher Insider keeps you safe by getting you into action, so you can feel a sense of agency and control. Its opposite, Being, values presence, reflection and rest. The Pusher sees rest as dangerous, and will warn you not to slow down, because then you'll fall behind and never catch up. Being, on the other hand, looks at Pusher, and wonders where he's trying to get to in such a rush, when all the answers are right here, right now.

There's often a feeling of competition and one-upmanship between opposite characters. Insiders feel superior to their Outsider opposites, believing their approach is right, good, virtuous and wise. For example, Perfectionist's opposite is Messy. Perfectionist believes that to be good, you have to eliminate errors, create order and achieve flawless quality. Messy believes that to be good is to be spontaneous and free, and celebrates flaws as beautifully human and relatable. Each will fail to comprehend the others' world. Perfectionist might look at Messy's chaotic workspace and exclaim, "I don't know how you can work here," while Messy will look at Perfectionist's orderly, neat environment and feel stifled by its rigidity.

The work of the Inner Leader is to find the both/and balance. It does this by recognizing the importance of both sides of these inner polarities, appreciating and including the perspectives of each. For Pusher and Being, this might look like taking action with presence rather than rushing through tasks; or taking breaks to rest to re-energize yourself for action. For Perfectionist and Messy, this might look like setting a standard of good enough, and relaxing into the "messy middle" of projects.

4. CHARACTERS REACT LIKE REAL PEOPLE

The idea that characters are like whole people is more than a playful way of visualizing our inner world. It's actually a useful guideline for you (the Inner Leader) to follow, because it reminds you that you are always in relationship with your characters.

You can relate to them judgmentally, ignore them, attach negative labels to them, even exile them from your awareness altogether. Or you can turn towards them with curiosity, include them, consult them, actively invite their participation. The former breaks trust with these characters, the latter builds it. The more you listen to a character's concerns and suggestions, the more they will trust you, and be amenable to your direction when you need them to take a step back.

Just like real people, the characters on your Inner Team want to be seen, valued, and included. When they are included and consulted, you'll have access to their insights, perspectives and wisdom. When they feel judged by you, they will sometimes go silent, denying you their gifts.

Or they may get louder and more demanding until you pay attention to what they have to say, showing up in extreme ways which makes their gifts harder to see.

5. CHARACTERS TEAM UP AND WORK COOPERATIVELY

Every character wants to protect you, and has a strategy which works in certain situations. Got a deadline approaching? Your Pusher will get you into action, and keep you going until the task is done. Got an angry customer? Your Pleaser will help you identify precisely what they need from you.

But what happens when that strategy isn't sufficient to meet the challenge? They call a friend.

Characters form partnerships, and work cooperatively to keep you safe. Here are some common combinations:

Pleaser and Pusher: Pleaser tells you that it's essential to meet others' expectations, Pusher will drive you to check off every task on the to-do list which is necessary to meet or exceed their expectations.

Perfectionist and Responsible: Perfectionist sets the standard that your work must be error free, the Responsible keeps you making steady, incremental progress until it's done.

Independent and Rational: Independent say you must rely on no-one but yourself to make decisions, Rational does the thinking to ensure the decision is logical.

Playful and Being: Playful sets course for fun, Being allows you to stay present enough to really enjoy it.

Spiritual and Boundaried: Spiritual seeks inner peace and the experience of connectedness, Boundaried manages your schedule to ensure you have time to get still and be present.

While every character operates as if they have the <u>best</u> way to keep you safe, they will form partnerships with other characters who do not directly contradict this approach. This contradiction happens most frequently with opposites, whose approach to keep you safe is radically different. But some characters who are not direct opposites are nevertheless quite suspicious of each other. Perfectionist, for example, is <u>most</u> threatened by Messy's experimental, chaotic way of being, but it's also quite worried about Being, because it's dangerous to rest, chill out and take naps when a task is not yet finished to a satisfactory standard.

6. ALL CHARACTERS ARE TRYING TO PROTECT THE VULNERABLE CHILD

The Vulnerable Child is a universal character, because it's where we all begin: dependent on others to meet our needs, acutely sensitive to what's going on around us, unable to function independently.

For all of the adult capacities we develop as we mature, this tender and sensitive part is always within us, feeling everything deeply. It doesn't grow up to become more resilient, resourceful or confident. It stays forever powerless, frightened and overwhelmed.

When we say that every character on your Inner Team is trying to protect you, it's this Vulnerable Child within you that they're trying to keep safe. If your Vulnerable Child is particularly sensitive to being abandoned, characters such as the Pleaser will emerge to keep your relationships intact. If she's easily confused and disoriented, Rational will emerge to help her make sense of what's happening in the confusing world around you. If she's afraid of being powerless, characters like Warrior and Controller will emerge to protect her by fighting back.

The Vulnerable Child is the fulcrum of the entire Inner Team. Every dynamic reflects how characters are trying, in their own way, to keep her from feeling her most painful feelings.

Over time, your Inner Leader can learn to take over as the "inner parent" to your Vulnerable Child, which will allow the rest of your Inner Team characters to relax their grip on your behavior. Your responses to threats will become less compulsive, less reactive, and more conscious.

See chapter six for a more detailed description of the central role of the Vulnerable Child on your Inner Team, and what inner parenting looks like in practice.

PART 2
THE CAST OF CHARACTERS

"Every one of us has a thousand different kinds of little people inside of us. And some of them want to get out and be wild, and some want to be sad or happy or inventive or even just go dancing... And all those different little people inside of us? We must never be afraid to take them with us wherever we may go... who knows when we may need one of them to pop up and rescue us from ourselves? The great secret is not the variety of life, it's the variety of us."

FROM STAR TREK: THE NEXT GENERATION, SEASON 5, EPISODE 20 (CITED IN SCHWARTZ AND FALCONER, 2017, P.54)

CHAPTER 4

THE FIELD GUIDE
TO THE INNER TEAM

When you turn towards your inner world with curiosity, who might you encounter?

In theory, there are an infinite number of possible characters. In practice, however, certain characters emerge over and over again, across individuals of all ages and backgrounds. This section profiles fifty of the characters who frequently make their presence known on the Inner Team.

Each of these profiles has been developed from observation, reflection and practice with clients of Inner Team Dialogue and its precursor, Voice Dialogue. Think of them as composites of the self-observation of hundreds of seekers who've looked within themselves.

The profiles are presented in twenty four pairs (polarities) of opposite, interdependent characters. Two additional characters, the Inner Critic and the Vulnerable Child, are so crucially important that they get chapters of their own.

Every profile here is incomplete and partial. While you may

recognize certain traits of your characters in a description, others won't fit you at all. When your experience of a character and the descriptions in this book diverge, trust your own experiences.

PROFILE SECTIONS

With the exception of the Inner Critic and the Vulnerable Child, each character profile is organized into the following sections:

How the Character Protects You

Every character protects your vulnerability in a unique way. This section explores the nature of a characters protection, and in some cases, specific vulnerabilities that it protects.

How the Character Operates as an Insider

These descriptions attempt to capture what patterns of thought, feeling and behavior this character produces when it's playing a leading role on your Inner Team.

Origins of the Character

This section points towards the kind of early experiences which can lead to this character developing into an Insider. Consider these as examples only, not a definitive description of a character's origin.

How the Character Operates when Out of Balance with its Opposite

This section describes specific problems this character can cause when it is overused, without the moderating influence of its opposite.

Integration

This section describes what the "both/and" balance between a pair of opposite characters looks like.

JOURNALING ABOUT YOUR CHARACTERS

The journey of cultivating your Inner Leader begins with recognizing the characters within, and ultimately befriending them. The most consistently useful way to engage with this material, and deepen your understanding, appreciation and connection with your characters, is through journaling.

Here are some journaling prompts. For each character you choose to explore in yourself, turn your attention towards these areas, and write about your experience.

Activation Signals: Thoughts, emotions or sensations that indicate this character's activation

Rules of Behavior: What this character tells you to do, or not do.

Gifts: What do you appreciate about this character's role in your life?

Liabilities: What problems do you experience when you overuse this character?

Other reflections: What else are you noticing about this character's role in your life?

WHY NAME YOUR CHARACTERS?

Some other parts-work methods don't feature a nomenclature of named parts. So why do named characters feature so prominently in Inner Team Dialogue? The reasons are quite compelling:

"What the eye doesn't see and the mind doesn't know, doesn't exist."

This quote from an unlikely source (D.H. Lawrence in <u>Lady Chatterley's Lover</u>) captures the single biggest benefit of naming your characters. What you name, you notice.

Names like Pleaser or Perfectionist are in common parlance. As a direct result of this many people can readily identify these characters in themselves. But it would be a rare person who has a name for the part of themselves which turns mountains into molehills (Minimizer), or the part which thrives in chaos (Messy). They're less well-known, but of equal importance.

A Useful Shorthand

Naming is a shorthand, a way of quickly capturing something complex. It's far easier to say "My Pusher is activated" than to list all of the somatic and cognitive evidence that this is so: an urgent sense of needing to get somewhere, which turns your attention away from people and towards tasks, accompanied by muscle tension in the neck and jaw.

A Shared Vocabulary

Your Pusher and my Pusher may have some individual differences, but they're substantially alike. A common name confirms that other people experience many of the same kinds of thoughts, feelings and sensations that you do. This awareness alone often produces a feeling of relief that you're not alone.

A Positive Frame

I used to refer to my Being character as "The Slob".... hardly a complimentary way of labeling the part of me that honors the importance of rest. Negatively-slanted names create barriers to seeing our characters as the protective influences that they are. Giving positive names to parts helps ensure that we're talking about these amazing characters in a way that they find welcoming and inclusive.

"Name It to Tame It"

Neuroscientist Dr. Dan Siegel coined the term "name it to tame it" to describe what happens when we label a strong emotion. Brain imaging studies demonstrate that when we activate the part of the brain which produces language (the prefrontal cortex), there is a reduction in activity in the emotion-generating regions of the brain, specifically the amygdala. Naming a character seems to have a similar, somewhat calming effect.

Granularity and Nuance

There are several characters which are somewhat alike. For example, Expert and Judge have a major trait in common: believing that you know enough to form an opinion and be confident in its rightness. But they show up differently, and the distinctions between them are meaningful and useful. Having a wide range of character names is a bit like having a broad, nuanced vocabulary to describe your emotions.

Caveat: The Name Itself Doesn't Matter

Having listed all the reasons why naming is helpful, there's one important caveat. It doesn't actually matter what you call them, as long as it's both positive and memorable for you. It doesn't have to make sense to anyone else. The act of naming is more important than the name itself. For example, one Inner Team Dialogue client renamed her Being character "Peaceful", because this is how she experiences herself when Being is activated. Another called the same character "Beach Cottage" because that's where she was most able to live in the moment, rest and reflect.

WHICH CHARACTERS SHOULD I GET TO KNOW?

Among the fifty characters featured in this book, how do you choose where to start your explorations?

It can be helpful to use a problem or challenge you are currently experiencing as a pointer towards characters which might be relevant to your development.

PROBLEM OR CHALLENGE	CHARACTERS TO EXPLORE
Aloof	Rational, Observer, Boundaried
Analysis paralysis	Rational, Perfectionist
Arrogant	Judge, Rational, Special, Expert
Bored / disengaged / uninspired	Responsible, Pragmatist
Burnout / exhaustion	Pusher, Pleaser, Responsible, Competitor
Can't switch off	Pusher, Thrill Seeker
Commitment problems	Free Agent, Messy, Playful
Controlling, domineering, dictatorial	Controller, Patriarch, Competitor, Planner
Deferential	Pleaser, Rule Follower, Peacemaker
Defiant, oppositional	Rebel, Special, Protector
Disorganized	Messy, Playful, Improviser
Distrustful	Protector
Dreamy, ungrounded	Being, Spiritual
Driven / intense	Pusher, Competitor
Frustrated	Protector, Warrior, Pusher
Hyper-ambitious	Competitor, Pusher

Hyper-critical of others	Judge, Perfectionist
Hyper-rational	Rational Mind, Boundaried
Hyper-sensitive	Vulnerable Child, Maximizer
Image conscious	Perfectionist, Special
Impatient	Pusher, Competitor
Inflexible, resistant to change	Protector, Judge, Comfort Seeker
Judgmental	Judge, Rational, Special
Naive	Trusting
Non-collaborative	Independent, Rebel, Competitor
Non-reflective	Expert/Knower, Comfort Seeker, Zebra
Over-adaptable, accommodating	Pleaser, Peacemaker, Chameleon
Over-empathic	Pleaser, Feeling
Over-indulging	Indulger, Thrill Seeker
Over-serious, not having any fun	Responsible, Rational, Rule Follower, Restrictor
Overconfidence	Knower, Special
Overfocus on details (nitpicky)	Perfectionist, Judge
Passive aggressive	Pleaser, Controller, Peacemaker
Perfectionist	Perfectionist, Inner Critic
Poor listener	Expert, Patriarch, Judge
Procrastination	Being, Dependent, Comfort Seeker, Protector
Reactive	Protector, Warrior
Risk-averse, "playing safe"	Protector, Controller, Comfort-Seeker, Maximizer
Risk-taking	Thrill Seeker, Trusting, Rebel
Self-critical	Inner Critic
Self-effacing	Ordinary, Pleaser, Minimizer
Success amnesia	Inner Critic, Minimizer, Pusher
Unwilling to delegate	Controller, Independent, Pusher
Victim	Dependent, Vulnerable Child

Withholding communication	Observer, Peacemaker, Pleaser,
Won't ask for help	Independent
Worry/anxiety about others	Pleaser, Responsible
Worry/anxiety about self	Protector, Victim/ Hypochondriac, Vulnerable Child

ARTIST AND PRAGMATIST

Integrating the Artist and the Pragmatist allows you to balance:
- Beauty **and** functionality
- Creating something new **and** making use of what already exists
- The transcendent **and** the everyday

THE ARTIST
The Artist is the part of each of us which has an irresistible desire to imagine, create, express yourself and make the world a little more beautiful.

How the Artist Protects You
The Artist carries your instinctual urge to create. Its energy is unconstrained, unpredictable and irrepressible. It is a source of aliveness, and a source of restoration when you're depleted.

While the Artist will tell you that creating is an end in itself, it is one of the most constructive outlets for you to process your emotions. Art can be transformational, having the capacity to transmute pain into beauty.

The Artist Insider
The Artist Insider most commonly finds its expression through work in the creative arts, but it can bring imagination and creativity to any domain of life. It powers the capacity to generate new ideas, to innovate, to see what could be rather than focusing on what is.

The Artist commonly identifies beauty as a core value. Nothing offends this character more than a lack of creativity, for example in a building that's functional but ugly, or a blank wall that could be a canvas for a mural.

The most common expression of the Artist is by creating. It doesn't have to be art in the traditional sense, it can emerge as creating a meal, creating an elegant plan for your vacation, or creating an experience for guests at a party. Whatever the Artist touches, it brings a refined sensitivity, particularly to aesthetics. The Artist won't allow you to produce a piece of work that is purely functional: it will express something about you, and feature visual or creative flair.

The Artist has an energy that is not easily contained. It can emerge in an oppositional form, pushing against convention, rules, structures and traditions, or in the impulse to try something completely new. Whatever form it takes, the Artist sees life as a search for voice, for authenticity, for expression of what's true in the moment.

Because the Artist likes generating reactions from others, it can be mistaken for the Warrior. Both like to be provocative; the difference is that the Warrior is trying to experience themselves as powerful, where the Artist is trying to experience themselves as a creative force who can bring something new into the world. To the Artist Insider, it's infinitely preferable to generate a negative reaction than to be met with indifference. Being greeted with silence or being ghosted can be particularly hot buttons for this character.

The Origins of the Artist

The Artist represents an archetype which everyone has access to. Its most vigorous expression is often in children. When a child's creative urge is nurtured, the Artist will continue to operate in its uniquely generative way, growing throughout life. When the child's creative product (their painting, sculpture, even their fort made of pillows and blankets) is criticized, the Artist can become an Outsider. While it can be repressed, it is always there, waiting for permission to emerge, even in people who label themselves as "not creative".

The Artist can also come to prominence on the Inner Team for people who feel silenced or misunderstood. For example, think of the moody teenager putting their tortured emotions on paper as poetry.

When the Artist is operating on the Inner Team without the balancing influence of the Pragmatist, you may experience:

- A tendency to be easily bored, or an aversion to repetition and routine
- Prioritizing beauty over all other factors (e.g. a beautiful outfit that's too uncomfortable to wear, a beautifully decorated space that is difficult to use for its intended purpose)
- Inertia: an unwillingness to take action until you feel inspired
- A difficulty with compromise, especially around how things should look.

THE PRAGMATIST

The Pragmatist is the part of each of us which is straightforward, practical and grounded.

How the Pragmatist Protects You

The Pragmatist will guide you towards the simplest and most direct way to achieve an outcome. It's unerringly practical, sensible and uncomplicated. When you're overthinking, confused, or disoriented, the Pragmatist will simplify the problem for you. When your anxiety has you perseverating over a future problem, the Pragmatist will bring you back to the here and now, so you can focus on the next step.

The Pragmatist has a limited time horizon. It is focused on what needs to happen right now, and rarely looks far beyond this. The Pragmatist wants you to survive, and is largely uninterested in whether you thrive. Abstractions like "self-actualization" mean little to this character.

The Pragmatist is consistently resourceful. It can make a meal with whatever you have in your fridge. It can repair a machine with whatever you have in your garage. It doesn't waste energy worrying about what's missing, and gets on with making the best of what you do have.

The Pragmatist Insider

When the Pragmatist is an Insider on your Inner Team, you focus on function rather than form. You don't care how something looks, as long as it gets the job done. For the Pragmatist, design is all about making something work well, not making it look pretty. The Pragmatist is often notably blind to aesthetic considerations. If your old vehicle still gets you from A to B, you'll keep driving it. So what if it has a few scratches, dents and a different colored panel or two?

The Pragmatist Insider has a helpful kind of tunnel vision: it finds the shortest route to achieving a goal. It can tune out noise, and focus on signal. It produces a kind of practicality, a no-nonsense attitude, a willingness to just get on with it. It celebrates the methodical, deliberate, determined, and dismisses anything or anyone it considers flighty or fluffy.

The Pragmatist refuses to re-invent the wheel. If a solution already exists, the Pragmatist will use it. It was probably someone with a Pragmatist Insider who likely coined the phrase, "If it ain't broke, don't fix it." For this reason, the Pragmatist Insider can be both resistant to change and skeptical of innovation.

The Pragmatist Insider identifies a single objective, and tunes out everything else. For example, it will identify the purpose of eating as fueling the body with sufficient calories, and make food choices which accomplish this goal most efficiently, perhaps choosing a jar of peanut butter and a spoon as a more efficient calorie delivery mechanism than a fancy plated meal with pretty decorative garnishes.

Origins of the Pragmatist

The Pragmatist comes to prominence on the Inner Team out of necessity. When time and resources are limited, you do what has to be done with whatever you've got. It embodies the virtues of practicality and resourcefulness. It's a common adaptation to environments with overwhelming and endless demands, such as caring for a large family, or maintaining the livestock or crops on a farm.

There is sometimes a history of having been harmed or disappointed by people who talk a good game, weave clever narratives, but cannot deliver.

When the Pragmatist is operating on your Inner Team without the balancing influence of the Artist, you may experience:

- Dismissiveness towards anything that you label "impractical": art, music, spirituality, even liberal arts education.

- Disinterest in any area which involves creativity, innovation, imagination or dreaming
- Over-indexing on the present, to the exclusion of planning for the future.
- A difficulty seeing value in anything abstract or theoretical

CHAMELEON AND ZEBRA

Integrating Chameleon and Zebra allows you to balance:

- Adaptation to others **and** authenticity to yourself
- Mirroring **and** contrasting
- Blending in **and** standing out

THE CHAMELEON
The Chameleon is the part of each of us which is able to read social cues, mimic behavior and blend in

How the Chameleon Protects You

The Chameleon protects you from the vulnerability of not belonging or fitting in, and the associated fear of abandonment or rejection. It protects you against the fear that your true self will not be accepted.

The Chameleon's wants you to be able to fit in anywhere, with anyone. It helps you channel your empathy to attune to what's normal, praised, expected or judged in a given environment.

The Chameleon warns against the dangers of being too transparent. It believes that if you allow your authentic feelings, needs or agenda to be seen, you will be rejected, judged or stigmatized. It operates by the principle that the best way to get your needs met is by being able to assimilate into a group.

The Chameleon is often highly developed in people from minority or marginalized groups who have learned to fit in with dominant culture (code switching).

The Chameleon Insider

Like Woody Allen's character in the 1983 movie *Zelig*, for the Chameleon Insider, life is a constant effort to fit in, or not to stand out. Standing out feels threatening.

A Chameleon Insider is a shapeshifter, enabling you to flex and mold yourself to an audience. You may find yourself unconsciously mirroring others patterns of speech, body language, attitudes and priorities. The Chameleon's focus of attention is outside rather than inside yourself.

The Chameleon allows you to rapidly shift your way of being when you move between environments that have different expectations. It supports your ability to compartmentalize, for example, showing up as a different person at home, at work, or with friends.

The Chameleon is open to influence. It's the opposite of stubborn, demonstrating enormous flexibility and willingness to adapt. At its best, this character has an everyman quality, the ability to connect with anyone. It's common for sales professionals to be able to use their Chameleon to form relationship with a wide range of different customers. It's also well-developed in actors with a wide dramatic range, and politicians who can relate across tribal divides.

Chameleons are particularly skilled at making a positive first impression. Since imitation is the sincerest form of flattery, Chameleon's capacity to mimic can initially make others feel admired and validated. Over time, however, your Chameleon's preference for keeping yourself hidden can become an impediment to deeper, more lasting connection. The Chameleon will help you be who your partner needs you to be, but it can come across as performative or inauthentic. Chameleon struggles to show up in relationship as a consistent, steady, authentic presence. Over time, it can breed distrust.

The Chameleon's opinions are strongly influenced by the last person they spoke with. Julia Roberts' character in the 1999 movie *The Runaway Bride* is a great example. Asked "How do you like your eggs?" her answers describe how her previous partners liked their eggs. She is unable to answer about her own preferences.

Origins of the Chameleon

This character emerges quite early in development, because we learn to be part of a social group by mimicry. Socialization depends on the Chameleon.

Those with a particularly strong Chameleon often describe an early environment in which standing out was dangerous in some way, and blending in with a group was the way to be safe. It can also become over-active in children who move a lot, helping them fit in as they join new schools and adapt to different cultural norms.

Whatever unique circumstances led to the development of your Chameleon, it will reliably support you to read the room, and adapt fluently.

When the Chameleon is operating in your Inner Team without the balancing influence of the Zebra, you may experience:

- Inauthenticity – trying so hard to fit in that you lose connection with who you are

- Feeling unsure who you are, as you switch rapidly between personas

- By favoring assimilation rather than differentiation, you may withhold your unique contribution, in favor of being just like everyone else.

- At the extreme, Chameleons can be smooth liars. You may believe your own deceptions and lose contact with what's true.

THE ZEBRA

The Zebra is the part of you which will not change its stripes.

How Zebra Protects You

Zebra provides certainty about who you are. If you're the same everywhere, with everyone, not only will others be able to count on you, you will be able to count on yourself.

You likely do not have a strong desire to fit in and be accepted. It's more important to you to be yourself. Your behavior will express what you think and feel; you don't filter yourself. Brene Brown captures this approach perfectly: *"True belonging doesn't require that we change who we are; it requires that we be who we are."*

The Zebra Insider

If the Zebra is an Insider on your Inner Team, you do not change yourself to fit in with any group. You are who you are, and you refuse to compromise yourself by pretending to be otherwise. You trust your own advice. You know yourself best. Your personal values feel like absolutes. Compromise feels like self-betrayal.

The Zebra operates by the WYSIWYG principle: What You See is What You Get.

Zebra Insiders are unpolished. They place minimal importance on others' impressions. This is not to say Zebra Insiders do not need to belong, simply that they accomplish this by being fully and unapologetically themselves. They send the message,

"This is who I am: take it or leave it."

Zebra Insiders can be critical of anything they interpret as fake. They're suspicious of those who follow trends and fashions, and anyone who they see as pandering to a crowd. To the Zebra Insider, trust is earned by reliability, consistency and directness. If you're not having a good time at a party, for example, you're more likely to leave than to put on a fake smile. If you dislike someone, you will not keep this hidden. You are likely to be a terrible liar.

Origins of the Zebra

The Zebra comes to prominence on the Inner Team when you have tried but failed to fit in. Feeling ill-equipped to be the kind of person who could fit in with others, you gave up trying, and adopted the opposite approach.

The Zebra can also come to prominence on the Inner Team as a reaction to being caught in a lie, or otherwise "found out". The Zebra is one reaction to this shaming experience, to ensure that this will never happen again.

Whatever the unique circumstances in your early environment, the Zebra produces a kind of stable, consistent way of being in the world which guards against being seen as fake, dishonest or flaky.

When the Zebra is operating in your Inner Team without the balancing influence of the Chameleon, you may experience:

- Social and interpersonal inflexibility. Largely uninterested in others expectations, you may be unwilling to adjust to the norms of a social group.

- Missing social cues, and a tendency to be socially tone deaf. You aspire to be the same in every setting, so you may not notice when this way of being does not fit the moment.

- Difficulty compartmentalizing, showing up the same way at home, at work, with friends.

- Difficulty with articulating a point of view other than your own.

COMFORT SEEKER AND THRILL SEEKER

Integrating Comfort Seeker and Thrill Seeker allows you to balance:

- Security **and** Adventure
- Familiarity **and** Newness
- Nurturing yourself **and** Challenging yourself

THE COMFORT SEEKER

Comfort Seeker is the part of each of us which responds to a dangerous, unpredictable world by retreating into what's comfortable and familiar.

How the Comfort Seeker Protects You

No character is better equipped to help you wind down an over-stimulated nervous system, to re-stabilize you when you're thrown off balance. The Comfort Seeker's protective intent is to cushion you against emotional, physical and spiritual discomfort. It worries that you won't be able to cope with difficult feelings or external challenges. It wants to direct your attention away from them, into experiences it knows you can handle. It interprets discomfort as a sign to stop.

The Comfort Seeker is like an indulgent inner parent, who meets your sadness or fear with a cookie, and lets you stay home watching TV rather than taking the difficult math test at school.

The Comfort Seeker tries to create an inner sense of peace by withdrawing from that which disturbs. It imbues objects and routines in the external world with the magical power to provide peace and comfort.

PART OF ME

The Comfort Seeker Insider

When Comfort Seeker is operating as an Insider, you are likely to have many strategies to restore a sense of stability, familiarity and safety. Comfort food. A favorite pillow. Words of reassurance you repeat to yourself. An action you always perform at the same time, to give your day a familiar rhythm. Anything which distracts your attention from difficult feelings or hard decisions could be a strategy arising from your Comfort Seeker.

If the Comfort Seeker is an Insider on your Inner Team, your comfort zone will be hard to leave. This can look like doing only what you know you can do well, such as repeating a familiar exercise, or cooking the same meal over and over again. It can look like distracting yourself from difficult issues with whatever occupies your mind, from social media to a tv show, from a video game to a favorite book.

It will argue against trying a new item on a menu, when there's a familiar option available. It will persuade you not to try a new, unfamiliar form of exercise. It will suggest you stay at home rather than go out and make new connections. It will have you skip past a contrary political opinion in your news feed so you can remain in your comfortable echo-chamber. It will minimize your spiritual doubt when it brings your long-professed faith into question.

The Comfort Seeker Insider would rather you were numb than upset, because the absence of difficult feelings is its primary measure of success. Whether or not you feel actively good (joyful, vital, grateful, loving) is not its concern.

Origins of the Comfort Seeker

If your early experiences created a deep fear of failure, the Comfort Seeker rescues you from this by ensuring you never

68

attempt something unfamiliar or risky.

Over-protective parents may have led to you internalizing the message that you can't handle hard things. Your Comfort Seeker reinforces this belief, and keeps you in the comfort zone of easy, unchallenging experiences.

If your early experience featured a harsh, critical environment where external comfort wasn't available, your Comfort Seeker may have developed to offer you strategies for self-comforting.

Whatever circumstances brought it to prominence on your Inner Team, the Comfort Seeker protects the young, vulnerable little girl or boy within who can't cope with the confusing, unpredictable world, and wants to feel safe.

When Comfort Seeker is operating on your Inner Team without the balancing influence of Thrill Seeker, you may experience:

- Feeling "comfortably numb", stagnant, in a rut, apathetic and disinterested

- A feeling of fragility, believing you will be unable to cope with small changes in routine or new experiences.

- A day-to-day experience which lacks aliveness, is bereft of surprises.

- Relationships which are characterized by fake harmony, focusing on what's working rather than what's not.

- Interpreting all stress as something to be avoided. You may struggle to embrace the ways some stress can be useful as a prompt to development ("Eustress").

- Hesitancy to initiate change yourself, and a default resistance to change, expressed passively (through stubbornness or denial).

THRILL SEEKER (ADVENTURER)

The Thrill Seeker is the part of each of us which wants to experience aliveness, challenge and new experiences.

How it Protects You

The Thrill Seeker protects the part of you that's worried that your needs won't be met. It fears that you will be trapped in pain, isolation, missing out on all that life has to offer. Its job is to keep you from feeling this, which it accomplishes by keeping your attention focused on the next opportunity for excitement. It generates an insatiable desire for the next high, the next adventure, the next thrilling experience.

The Thrill Seeker protects you against feeling bored, and helps you escape feelings that rise to the surface when your mind is quieter, and your senses less stimulated. There is often an aversion to meditative and mindfulness practices. The Thrill Seeker will compulsively fill up your calendar with activities to crowd out feelings of vulnerability, disorientation or purposelessness.

Although Thrill Seeker and Comfort Seeker are opposites, they do have one strategy in common: they both distract your attention from difficult feelings. Comfort Seeker does this by numbing-out in routines, Thrill Seeker does this by creating intense, sometimes dangerous experiences that demand 100% of your attention and focus.

The Thrill-Seeker Insider

If the Thrill Seeker is an Insider on your Inner Team, you may be easily bored and prone to restlessness, disinterested with the familiar, habitual, or routine. The Thrill Seeker wants you to have first-hand experience rather than the vicarious experience of reading a book or watching a movie. It loves novelty, and is drawn to exploring the unknown, delighting in the feeling of anticipation of adventures to come, of discoveries to be made.

The Thrill Seeker Insider lives for sensation, the more intense the better. It can get hooked on the adrenaline rush that comes with taking a risk. It encourages over-doing all kinds of activities to produce this delicious feeling. It could be from riding your bike just a little too fast, having one drink too many, voicing a risky comment in a meeting, or metaphorically poking the bear. Counter-intuitively, the Thrill Seeker can also produce procrastination, enjoying the intensity of working under time pressure to hit a fast-approaching deadline.

Thrill Seeker lives in the question, "What will happen if I...." It is drawn towards experiences like speeding, sexual experimentation, gambling, extreme sports, high-risk investments, roller-coasters, and scary movies. At the extreme, the Thrill Seeker can generate the addictive pattern of the "adrenaline junkie" who seeks ever more thrilling experiences.

In the career domain, the Thrill Seeker prefers jobs which provide a high level of risk and challenge, and a steady stream of new challenges to confront. You'll find the Thrill Seeker as an Insider among serial entrepreneurs, turn-around consultants, firefighters (literal and metaphorical), and in many high-risk roles.

In relationships, the Thrill Seeker brings fun and excitement, but may struggle with feeling limited by a partner's needs, and tolerating the repeating, everyday rhythms of long-term relationship.

Origins of the Thrill Seeker

If your parents were fearful and hyper safety conscious or generally afraid of the world, and you experienced this as radically limiting your freedom, the Thrill Seeker can emerge as a reaction against these restrictions, a reflexive impulse to break safety rules, to embrace risk, to go all-in.

When the world you grow up in offers little opportunity for stimulation and excitement, the Thrill Seeker can emerge to fuel your imagination, dreaming of a future adventure. The prospect of a pleasure in future can relieve the pain and frustration of a dull present moment.

When the adults in your early environment could not be with emotions like sadness, grief or hopelessness, the Thrill Seeker emerges with a solution: express joy, excitement and fun instead.

Whatever circumstances brought it to prominence on your Inner Team, the Thrill Seeker protects the young, vulnerable little girl or boy within who fears being deprived or trapped in boredom or pain.

If Thrill Seeker is operating in your Inner Team without the balancing influence of the Comfort Seeker, you may experience:

- A compulsive seeking for pleasure and excitement, almost to the point of obsession.

- A fear of being bored, and an inner restlessness that's never satisfied.

- A need for speed, leading to a devaluing of aspects of human experience which have a naturally slower cadence (spiritual practice, reflection, even long-term relationships)

- Prioritizing based on what's the most fun or exciting, rather than any other criteria.

COMPETITOR AND COLLABORATOR

Integrating Competitor and Collaborator allows you to balance:
- Individual victory **and** collective progress
- My needs **and** our needs

THE COMPETITOR
The Competitor is the part of each of us which has a single-minded focus on winning.

How the Competitor Protects You
When winning is an all-consuming focus, it creates a kind of tunnel vision, in which only the finish line holds your attention. It's a highly effective way of distracting you from dealing with pain, or from domains of life where there's no clear definition of what it means to win.

The Competitor strives to earn you the spoils of victory, and guard you against the pain of losing, and the loss of social status which goes with it. Whether the financial rewards of winning a competitive bid at work, or the bragging rights from winning a game of Mario Kart with a friend, this character equates victory with worth.

The Competitor's intense focus on winning has its own inherent rewards. More than any other character, it produces focused attention and effort, and the capacity to tune out distractions.

The Competitor Insider
To the Competitor, the world is made up of winners and losers. You are either improving and getting ahead, or declining and falling

behind. As a result, this character turns <u>everything</u> into a competition. This generates intense drive, urgency, and a single-minded focus on being better than others. Few other characters can match the degree of motivation of an activated Competitor, facing down a challenger. The fiercer the Competition, and the greater the risk of losing, the more active and intense this character becomes. The Competitor is animated by a Darwinist certainty there can be only one winner in the battle for survival or status.

With a Competitor Insider, the fear of losing can be even stronger and more motivating than the desire to win. Failing to win isn't just disappointing, it's experienced as shameful. When this character is your Insider, the label "loser" feels like the worst possible insult. The Inner Critic is a near-inevitable partner for the Competitor, and will reliably undermine your worth when your result is anything other than first place. The ugly saying, "second place is the first loser," captures the Competitor/Inner Critic team.

As an Insider, this character seeks competitions which have a clear definition of winning, from competing to get the most likes on a social media post to racing to beat a personal best on the running track. It's this character who has the impulse to negotiate a lower price, even if you can afford the higher one, just for the satisfaction of having "won" the negotiation. It will activate to help you achieve a measurable goal, but isn't much interested in more nebulous aspirations like feeling rested or balanced.

The Competitor's tendency to turn everything into a competition with winners and losers can put a major strain on relationships. Winning an argument with your spouse is, after all, a hollow victory. The Competitor will even assert an opinion you don't necessarily believe, simply because it seems more likely to win over the other person. No other character is as prone to engaging in pointless power struggles. The Competitor's desire to prevail in any conflict, even around the most trivial issues, can temporarily crowd out all other considerations, like the impact on the other person when they "lose".

The most extreme version of this pattern turns other people into mere objects in the game you're playing, to be cared about only when they help you win, otherwise discarded and overlooked. If others suffer, that's acceptable collateral damage from achieving the victory. You are simply a player on the board, to be moved around so I can win the game. What happens to you is not my concern.

The Competitor struggles with the idea that everyone can be a winner. It's this character who tends to disparage a youth sports coach who gives out participation trophies to every kid. Winning must be difficult to achieve, or it is devalued (and so are you).

The Competitor is one of several Inner Team characters which can be extraordinarily single minded. At the extreme, this character can produce Machiavellian behavior, in which the end justifies the means, and ethical considerations are overlooked.

Origins of the Competitor

The Competitor tends to come to prominence in situations where there are limited resources (money, love, attention), and you must prevail over others to get your needs met.

It can also emerge from families who are highly ambitious for their children, driving them to excel. In these highly conditional environments, love is earned by achievements; there is no such thing as unconditional love.

When the Competitor is operating in your Inner Team without the balancing influence of the Collaborator, you may experience:

- One-upping others in conversation.

- A core belief the world is a dangerous place, where your survival is always at risk, and you must fight to get your needs met.

- Over-reliance on competitiveness as a source of motivation, to the exclusion of all other sources, such as a sense of higher purpose.

- An intense fear of losing, leading you to conceal any evidence that this occurred. The concealment can be from others (for example, omitting an unsuccessful career chapter from your resume) or yourself (claiming moral or pyrrhic victories).

- The belief that there can only be one winner produces othering of "them" (the competition). It's not enough to win, others have to lose.

- Working alone in order to receive all the credit for a success, even when collaboration would have been faster or more successful.

- Avoiding any activity in which there is no way to win.

- Experiencing compromise as a defeat.

THE COLLABORATOR

The Collaborator is the part of each of us which forms partnerships and alliances for mutual benefit.

How the Collaborator Protects You

The Collaborator's protective strategy is to form alliances, to join with others to get your needs met. It operates from a belief that together we are infinitely stronger than apart. This character is cooperative, believing there will be enough for everyone if we work towards a common goal.

The Collaborator lives in a world of "us" rather than "I". It is as community-oriented as the Competitor is individualistic. Its automatic preference to lean into support is highly protective against any feelings of isolation. It's a pro-social character, oriented to relationships, and driven by a sense of shared responsibility.

The Collaborator Insider
The Collaborator Insider is the ultimate team player, seeing the world through the lens of cooperation, partnership, and community. The Collaborator tends to move toward others, to form bonds, alliances, and agreements. It's characterized by sharing ideas and distributing ownership. It demonstrates a strong preference for consensus decision making.

Where the Competitor sees relationships as win vs lose, you vs me, the Collaborator rejects this framing, and creates partnerships to find solutions that serve everyone ("us versus the problem"). It's the Collaborator who will work tirelessly to balance personal needs with the needs of the other party, recognizing that win/lose solutions are inherently unstable and unlikely to sustain over time. Because of this interest in mutually beneficial solutions, the Collaborator tends to get activated by perceived inequality and unfairness.

This character is highly attuned to patterns of inclusion and exclusion. There's a deep empathy for the pain of being othered, excluded or marginalized, and a preference for creating inclusive groups. However, the need for consensus and harmony within groups is strong enough that this character will also enforce in-group and out-group boundaries, to keep less community-fo-cused individuals out, and ensure the health of the community as a whole.

Origins of the Collaborator

Because humans are social animals, the Collaborator is present to some degree in everyone. From the earliest lessons about the importance of sharing, this character is key to socialization. Without this character, it would difficult to prioritize the needs of the group over your own needs.

The Collaborator can come to prominence on the Inner Team when your early environment's value systems were more community-minded than individualistic.

It is often cultivated through participation in team sports, a context in which competitiveness and collaboration are both essential to success.

When the Collaborator is operating on your Inner Team without the balancing influence of the Competitor, you may experience:

- An over-reliance on consensus decision making, which can be both slow and prone to being hijacked by individual agendas.

- A tendency to avoid or delay acting independently. There's a pattern of waiting until you're certain of others' support before you'll take action.

- A tendency to see competitiveness negatively, overlooking its benefits in generating engagement, and energizing action. This leads to a reluctance to compete, even when competi-tion might be an effective strategy to achieve a desired result.

EXPERT/CONFIDENT AND LEARNER/HUMBLE

Integrating Confident/Expert and Humble/Learner allows you to balance:

- Trusting what you know **and** Learning what you don't
- Knowledge **and** Doubt
- Certainty **and** Uncertainty

EXPERT/CONFIDENT

Expert/Confident is the part of each of us which is certain we can rise to meet whatever challenges we face.

How Expert/Confident Protects You

Expert/Confident is a source of belief that you understand what's going on. The amount of information or knowledge you have is secondary to your belief that you'll be able to figure it out. It is the antidote to paralyzing self-doubt, and uncertainty in the face of incomplete knowledge. It produces a powerful sense of authority.

Expert/Confident is the part of you that can puff out its chest and declare what will be so. It supports your ability to take a position, assert a point of view, and contribute to a discussion. It will draw conclusions based on available information, without being stopped by what is yet unknown.

Leading with this character often boosts social standing: we consistently promote and elect people with Expert/Confident Insiders, who have the capacity to make themselves and others believe that they have the answers.

The Expert/Confident Insider

For this character, confidence isn't earned as much as claimed. The Expert/Confident Insider confers an identity as a capable and resourceful person who can rise to meet any challenge.

The Expert/Confident Insider focuses on what you do know, and not on what you don't know. It supports your capacity to make decisions with incomplete information. It doesn't get hung up about gaps in knowledge, or conflicting information, and does not suffer from analysis paralysis.

Expert/Confident is the part of you who'll try to fix a broken appliance in your home, even when you don't know quite how to do it. It's the source of courage to apply for a job you're not 100% qualified for. It's the source of resilience to bounce back after a setback and try again.

It's easy to stereotype this character as an arrogant, strutting – and almost certainly male – figure convinced of his own mastery, only ever a moment away from launching into mansplaining. When out of balance with its balancing opposite, Humble, it can and does produce over-confidence, even arrogance. Expert/Confident will sometimes claim expertise it doesn't <u>yet</u> possess, but the belief that you'll be able to figure it out is a genuine superpower. It allows you to persist in the face of obstacles and setbacks, when others would fall victim to doubt, judge themselves as inadequate, throw up their hands and give up.

Expert/Confident will often adopt an identity as an expert, which is why it's part of the name for this character. It is near impossible to function in any expertise-based role without this character reinforcing that, however partial or incomplete your knowledge, you know <u>enough</u>. Without Expert/Confident, doubt would significantly constrain your capacity to contribute to the world around you.

When Expert/Confident adopts the social role of the expert, its most characteristic behavior is explaining. This character will latch on to any invitation to share what it knows, and will often do so at length. The Expert is a lecturer by nature. It can be extraordinarily generous in sharing knowledge, but often over-explains because it thinks every detail is important. If you can talk someone's ear off, long past the time their need for information has been met, it's likely the Expert/Confident character who is driving the explaining behavior.

Origins of Expert/Confident

Expert/Confident emerges as a solution to feeling lost, uncertain, confused or overwhelmed. Expert/Confident allows you to play big, even when you're feeling small. Better to claim to be an expert than to feel the vulnerability of feeling incapable or trapped.

It often comes to prominence in environments where showing weakness or uncertainty would have been dangerous. This is a common narrative for men, since many cultures shame men for revealing doubt or displaying fear. In cultures that demand it, Confident emerges as a way to rise to meet expectations of male dominance and potency. There is compelling research to show that men tend to over-rate their performance, such as Columbia Business School's study which found that men, on average, rated their performance <u>30 percent better than it was.</u> While it may be a more common Insider in a man's Inner Team, Confident is by no means only a male character. While men are <u>more</u> over-confident, research has found that women also demonstrate over-confidence, just to a slightly lesser degree.

When Expert/Confident is operating on your Inner Team without the balancing influence of Humble, you may experience:

- Arrogance, particularly the tendency to both over-estimate your own intelligence and insight, and to underestimate the intelligence of others.

- Overconfidence in yourself, leading to getting out of your depth.

- Lack of curiosity.

- A pattern of over-explaining, sharing your knowledge to prove how much you know (and cover up where you have gaps and doubts), even in situations where asking, co-exploring and listening would be more appropriate.

- A tendency to offer unsolicited advice.

- Exaggerating the breadth and depth of your knowledge.

HUMBLE/LEARNER

Humble/Learner is the part of each of us which knows how little we really know, and remains curious and open to learning.

How Humble Protects You

Humble/Learner keeps you from over-reaching your current capability. It's the antidote to overconfidence, moderating the feeling that you can achieve anything (like a teenager who's certain he can drive a car at high speed, despite being a brand-new driver). It offers a more cautious approach, preferring that you take in more information before you act.

Humble/Learner supports your capacity to learn and adapt. It keeps you open to taking in new information, even when it might contradict or challenge what you previously believed. It makes it possible to change your mind, preventing your thinking from becoming dogmatic and rigid.

It is easy to have a conversation with a person with a strong Humble/Learner character, because they will listen, be curious, really take in what you are saying. Where Confident/Expert will tend to make statements and share what it already knows, Humble/Learner is more likely to ask a question with the intent of learning something new. Humble's curiosity and openness deepen connections and strengthen relationships.

Humble/Learner also protects you by promoting the thought that you're not quite ready to begin. If you keep learning and studying, you never have to feel the vulnerability that comes from feeling out of your depth, or failing.

Humility is protective against shame, because it accepts rather than feels diminished by your flawed, imperfect human-ness. It will also keep narcissism in check, because it won't allow the idea that you're better than anyone else to pass unchallenged.

The Humble/Learner Insider

The Humble/Learner Insider creates an identity as a lifelong learner, by contrast with Expert/Confident, which forms an identity based on existing expertise. For Humble/Learner, existing knowledge is held lightly, seen as useful but incomplete.

Where the Confident/Expert character can be fragile when questioned, prone to defending their rightness, Humble/Learner does the exact opposite. When challenged or confronted with difference, this character gets curious, rather than feeling threatened by it. There is a marked intellectual flexibility, a willingness to consider new ideas, and a genuine curiosity about other points of view. Doubt and confusion are embraced as the starting point of learning and growth, rather than something which has to be fixed or resolved.

The Humble/Learner Insider thrives in diverse environments where there are many points of view and a wide range of opinions. It's quick to embrace the idea that there are many right answers, valid approaches or reasonable conclusions.

The Humble/Learner Insider is typically hesitant to form and declare conclusions. On the occasions where this character does share a point of view, it will include caveats and disclaimers ("The data is incomplete, and more research is needed, but here are our preliminary conclusions about what we think we might be seeing...") This communication pattern can come across as lacking in confidence, but it's more a reflection of a state of openness, a belief that knowledge is always incomplete and ever-evolving. Definitive conclusions are distrusted, because at best they represent only our current understanding.

Where Confident will feel the impulse to conceal gaps in knowledge, Humble/Learner is more likely to reveal them. Because this character feels no need to pretend to have everything figured out, it supports the capacity to ask for help, and to make fun of yourself.

Humble/Learner can be subject to a less well-known aspect of the Dunning-Kreuger effect. This cognitive distortion is typically associated with overestimating one's knowledge and capability, which is unsurprisingly a far greater risk for Confident/Expert than Humble/Learner. But the Dunning-Kreuger effect also includes a cognitive distortion where you believe you know

<u>less</u> than you really do. Humble/Learner is often so piercingly aware of what you don't know, or what can't be conclusively proven, that it can lead to understating your expertise.

Origins of Humble/Learner

Humble/Learner often emerges in cultures and family systems that carry strong negative judgments around arrogance and excessive pride. This can have many sources, from a reaction to a family member who demonstrated narcissism or entitlement, to a spiritual or religious belief.

Whatever the specific origins of your Humble/Learner character, it will enable you to engage with yourself and others in an open, modest, unassuming manner, learning everything you can.

When Humble/Learner is operating on your Inner Team without the balancing influence of Confident, you may experience:

- Underestimating the value of the knowledge and experience you already have, preferring the safety of deferring to "best practices" and external authorities.

- Delaying and procrastinating, never feeling ready to begin.
- Self-effacement, minimizing the importance of who you are and what you think, leading to withholding your contribution.

A Note on Humility and Expertise

These two characters react in opposite ways to the truth that knowledge is always partial and incomplete. Confident accepts that you'll never know it all, and concludes that what you know already is enough to form opinions and make decisions. Learner strives to always learn more, and focuses on filling in the gaps in knowledge. On first impression, Confident looks more expert, but over time people with a strong Humble character often develop more expertise than people with a strong Expert, because they never stop learning.

Distinguishing Confident/Expert and Humble/Learner from Judge and Neutral

There is a significant overlap between these two pairs of characters, and they can be mistaken for each other.

Both Confident/Expert and the Judge operate from the premise that you already know enough. Where Confident uses this knowledge to support taking action; Judge uses this knowledge to evaluate and make decisions on worth and value.

Similarly, Humble/Learner and Neutral share an openness about the world, and a preference for gathering information. Humble/Learner uses this as a strategy to get better informed, to learn more. Neutral uses it as a strategy to remain open, to sit with what is rather than forming a fixed opinion.

CONTROLLER AND ALLOWER

Integrating Controller and Allower enables you to balance:

- Changing the things you can change **and** accepting what you cannot change
- Leading **and** following
- My way **and** other ways
- Resisting **and** yielding

THE CONTROLLER

The Controller is the part of each of us which tries to achieve a sense of power and agency through taking charge and asserting influence.

How the Controller protects you

A feeling of being in control of your life is directly correlated with both physical and psychological health. A lack of control is inherently vulnerable, if also unavoidable. Controller is the character that emerges to address this vulnerability by striving for control. While there is considerable variation in the amount of perceived control required to feel safe, everyone uses some of the strategies of the Controller, at least some of the time.

The desire to achieve a sense of control can be expressed in any domain, from attempting to control your environment, your thoughts, your emotions, or the behavior of other people.

Whatever its expression, the Controller equates being in control with being safe, and experiences a lack of control as acutely threatening. This character is activated by experiences of feeling powerless, controlled or dominated by other people or adverse circumstances.

To counteract this fear, the Controller seeks, claims and exercises power, in whatever form it is available. It is the part of you that takes charge so that you experience yourself as having agency. This character is a source of strength, determination and force. It will fight rather than freeze or flee. Even in situations where you have little real control, it will find something it can control. The Controller is committed to eliminating all traces of passivity and complacency, which it experiences as dangerously close to surrender.

The challenge for this character is that, no matter how much power you claim and control you exercise, you are never fully in control of what happens in your life. Nevertheless, this character keeps score, and even determines your sense of worth, by how successfully you have controlled outcomes, from preventing problems to achieving results by sheer force of will.

The Controller Insider

Everyone needs a measure of control over their own lives, but the Controller Insider turns a need to feel in control into an identity, a primary measure of your worth.

Your Controller has the superpower of focus. When this character is activated, it can feel as if there is only one safe outcome, and you must make every conceivable effort to achieve it. The Controller narrows your focus, sometimes to the point of obsession. While this can be a tremendous source of energy and drive for achievement, it can blind you to other equally valid approaches to achieving a desired outcome.

In the professional domain, a Controller Insider will gravitate towards positions of formal authority, because being the boss feels safer than taking direction from others. Even if you do not seek positional power, you will likely exhibit a strong preference for roles in which you have substantial personal autonomy.

The Controller Insider creates a distinctive pattern of relationship within the workplace. This character's high control, directive approach has the unintended impact of producing dependency in those you lead. You want people to take direction from you (ideally without questioning you), but you simultaneously get frustrated that they do not seem to demonstrate much initiative. You may mistake compliance for agreement, silence for consent.

A similar pattern can show up in parenting too, where you expect your children to be obedient, but get frustrated that they don't act independently of your directives.

The Controller can leave you feeling isolated and unsupported, because others have learned that you will initiate, take charge, plan and act; they don't have a lift a finger. This further reinforces the Controller's belief that if you don't do it yourself, it won't get done.

The Controller Insider will often be the first to speak up in a group. It's safer to be the one who determines what is talked about than to respond to whatever someone else may wish to bring forward. Controllers' communication leans heavily on statements and demands, and does not ask many questions or invite debate.

The Controller's need for control in order to feel safe produces a "my way or the highway" pattern in relationships. This restricts the self-expression and assertion of your partner, and can create power struggles. Your partner may appreciate your willingness to initiate, but left unchecked, your Controller can crowd them out, making them feel that their participation and input are neither needed nor valued. Paradoxically, the more you attempt to control, the more resistance you are likely to face.

Origins of the Controller

There are usually past experiences of feeling out of control, being denied agency or choice. You decided that you would never let yourself feel powerless again, and you would demand and claim control for yourself. The degree of control you aspire to is directly proportional to the degree of anxiety you feel about your powerlessness.

When the Controller is operating on your Inner Team without the Balancing influence of Allower, you may experience:

- Being very reactive when you feel out of control, unable to stay present when feeling this vulnerable emotion.

- The desire for control of your own life can drift into wanting control of the lives of others. In its most extreme form, this can look like manipulation, coercion or bullying to get your own way.

- Using ultimatums to compel compliance.

- Reluctance to share ownership or distribute authority, preferring to keep it all for yourself.

- A recurring narrative that others are trying to control you (which is projected).

- Insisting on having your way, denying others choice. Micro-managing yourself and others.

THE ALLOWER

The Allower is the part of each of us which finds safety in radical acceptance of what is occurring.

How the Allower Protects You

The Allower makes it possible to relax into the knowledge that you are never fully in control of what occurs in your life. It advocates that you resist nothing, believing that resistance is the source of suffering. In response to a challenge, the Allower will have you soften up rather than tense up, so you move with what is happening rather than fight it. If the Controller meets a challenge with will, force and resistance, Allower takes exactly the opposite position. It's more martial artist than boxer, moving with an attack rather than resisting it.

The Allower is an invaluable ally when facing circumstances that are beyond your control. For example, dealing with a medical condition, the impact of a natural disaster, or even the behavior of other people in your life. Rather than demanding that the world makes sense and conform to your needs or preferences, the Allower can release this need, and accept what is.

The Allower Insider

The Allower Insider adopts an approach to life that is distinctly counter-cultural, and is widely misunderstood. It rejects the personal growth narrative which advocates empowerment and taking charge of your life. Instead, it finds power in yielding, in surrender, in the capacity to move with rather than against the currents of life. Allowing is often conflated with being complacent or ineffectual, interpreted as evidence of a failure of courage. But this character represents a different kind of courage:

to be with what is, without judging, rejecting or feeling victimized by it.

Where the Controller believes change comes from exerting dominance over oneself, the Allower sees acceptance as the precondition of change. This position was perfectly articulated by psychologist Carl Rogers: "When I accept myself just as I am, then I can change."

The Allower makes space for curiosity about what is unfolding. Rather than wasting energy on unanswerable questions like "Why is this happening to me?", the Allower will redirect your attention to explore and feel into what is occurring, right now. It has little use for ideas of what *should* happen (e.g. bad things shouldn't happen to good people), preferring to focus on sensing what is happening, and responding to it.

The Allower Insider can often be found in people of deep faith, who use this character to support their capacity to surrender to what they understand as the will of the divine.

The Origins of the Allower

There is usually some experience of frustration with attempts to gain some control. Because control feels out of reach, the Allower emerges as an alternate, coherent response to a world that is disinterested in your comfort or desired outcomes.

For others, the Allower emerges when you realize that constantly trying to achieve control is depleting you. Trying to force the world to conform to your will is not only exhausting, it's endless. There's no point where you finally achieve a state of complete control. It simply doesn't exist.

When the Allower is operating on your Inner Team without the balancing influence of the Controller, you may experience:

- Passivity and fatalism, a feeling that there's no point doing anything, because it won't make any difference.

- Difficulty internalizing and acting on the distinctions of the famous serenity prayer ("God, grant me the serenity to accept the things I cannot change, the courage to change the things I can, and the wisdom to know the difference.").

INDEPENDENT AND DEPENDENT

Integrating Independent and Dependent allows you to balance:
- Giving **and** receiving
- Trusting myself **and** trusting others
- Pulling your weight **and** sharing the load

INDEPENDENT
Independent is the self-reliant part of each of us which can shoulder individual responsibility

How Independent Protects You
Independent protects you from the risk of relying on other people, whose support may be unreliable. Independent promotes the conviction that you don't need anyone else in order to be safe, that you are able to meet your own needs. Independent is the ultimate individualist.

For Independent, the feeling of needing and depending on others is experienced as unbearably vulnerable. Accepting help feels diminishing. Being a burden on others is shameful. Self-sufficiency and meeting your own needs, however, are a source of pride.

This character steels you to expect nothing, to protect you from being disappointed.

The Independent Insider
When this character is an Insider, you prioritize meeting your own needs, whenever possible. This character brings a clenched-jaw

determination to prove, over and over again, that you can do it yourself.

Self-reliance is not just an attitude for this character, it's a practice. Independent will make sure that whatever you might need, you come prepared, from extra snacks on a long hike to extra insurance when traveling.

This character wants to be seen as capable, and will sometimes try to bolster these perceptions with stories that illustrate its resourcefulness, independence and individual strength. Many people with an Independent Insider will have a "pulled myself up by my bootstraps" origin story.

Independent tends to be strong in entrepreneurs, innovators, and free thinkers. It bestows the gift of being willing to break from the crowd, choose your own direction, captain your own ship.

Independent values struggle as a way to build self-reliance, and can be judgmental of anything resembling rescuing. This is often evident in this character's approach to parenting, where kids are expected to rise to a challenge and figure things out for themselves.

The Independent Insider will rarely, if ever, ask for help. Working a problem yourself, without having to read directions or even watch an instructional video, is deeply satisfying. It's Independent who will stubbornly refuse to ask for directions, even when completely lost.

When help is offered, it's not unusual for this character to feel offended, as if the offer of help implies you are unable to complete a task yourself. The idea that others might *want* to help you, that it might make them feel needed and important, is unlikely to occur to this character. This is one manifestation of a pattern of not recognizing – or flatly denying - your interdependence.

This character typically experiences ambivalence about teamwork. Rather than feeling supported by others' assistance, Independent feels diminished by it. This leads to behaviors like going it alone rather than collaborating with others. A distrust of others' motives is common, as is a tendency to interpret an offer of support as an attempt to control and dominate. Freedom to act independently is fiercely defended.

At an extreme, this character can produce hoarding. When you carry a core belief that you are on your own, that no one will take care of your needs, it makes sense to hoard whatever resources you have. Holding onto money without ever spending anything on yourself is a common expression of the Independent character.

Like its close cousin, Responsible, this is a character that will step forward to take ownership. For Responsible, this is about keeping commitments to others; for Independent, it's about not imposing a burden on others.

Independent often partners with the Competitor to create a hyper-individualistic approach to life, in which you feel that it's all up to you, there's competition for scarce resources, and no one will be coming to help.

Origins of Independent

Independent often emerges when the adults in your early environment were unreliable at meeting your needs. This leads to the conclusion that you can't depend on anyone else. You'd better get busy meeting your own needs, because no one else will.

Independent also emerges when children are neglected, and forced to fend for themselves at an early age.

Independence is revered in the individualistic Western world. The mythology of the rugged individualist is persistent, and reinforced constantly in cultural narratives. You'll find evidence for this in the way we celebrate entrepreneurs and small business owners, for example. Anything that even hints at promoting dependence (like social safety net programs) engenders fierce criticism. These messages create the conditions for Independent to become an Insider and Dependent an Outsider across the society as a whole.

When Independent is operating on your Inner Team without the balancing influence of Dependent, you may experience: Denial of the ways in which you are supported by society (roads to drive on, law and order, education, etc.).

- Blind spots about how your actions impact others, and how others' actions impact you.

- Overwork, because you refuse to ask for help. For leaders, this can look like reluctance to delegate.

- Collapsing independence with worth, and seeing dependence as shameful.

- Taking on more than your fair share of labor (in a family or workplace)

DEPENDENT
Dependent is the part of each of us which can receive help and support.

How Dependent Protects You
Dependent is a universal character, because everyone starts life in a state of complete dependence, and remains dependent for

a long formative period. We live in a society in which we depend on other people for our basic survival, for clean water, food, law and order. Whether we like it or not, dependence is a reality of what it is to be human.

But in a society that worships independence, many people have a hard time seeing the Dependent character within themselves as positive. Independent will disparage Dependent as being weak, a taker, someone who'd rather sponge off others than earn their own way. Dependent's superpower is the counterpoint to this view: a constant awareness of the many ways in which we need each other, the web of interdependence on which we all depend for our survival.

Dependent protects you by allowing you to ask for and receive support from others. It serves as a buffer against isolation, the feeling that you are completely on your own, without help or support. It's the Dependent character who's behind the impulse to join, affiliate and belong.

The Dependent Insider

When Dependent is an Insider, you see yourself as inextricably linked to others. Your view of the world is collective rather than individualistic.

The openness to receiving support makes Dependent an essential contributor to healthy relationships of all kinds. Dependent is near the top of the list of the most relationship-focused characters, since it has no resistance to leaning into two-way, interdependent, mutually supportive relationships. Dependent makes collaboration and teamwork possible, because it always requires depending on each other. Without access to Dependent, there can be no interdependence.

When Dependent is an Insider, you will readily give credit to others, recognizing their unique contributions, without which your own accomplishments would not have been possible. The opposite pattern, in which you take credit for others' work or ideas, can indicate that Dependent is an Outsider.

Dependent is the part of you that will seek out a mentor, an AA sponsor, a support group, a doctor or a consultant, and receive their advice and support with grace and gratitude. The impulse to reach out for help is often prompted by the awareness that you can't do it on your own, that you need others' experience, expertise, resources, or connections.

When overused, Dependent can show up powerless, needy, weak and ineffectual, over-reliant on external direction. Dependent may idealize those who provide this support, fear their rejection, and seek their reassurance, creating relationships that have a parent-child dynamic.

Origins of Dependent

Dependent is a universal character, and is present in everyone. It tends to come to prominence on the Inner Team in cultures and family systems which prioritize the needs of the collective over the individual.

Dependent can emerge when parents are over-protective and are not willing to let their child struggle. The child receives the message that she is incapable of functioning independently.

When Dependent is operating on your Inner Team without the balancing influence of Independent, you may experience:

- A feeling of entitlement, that you deserve others' support and care (often accompanied by anger when it is not offered).

- Learned helplessness, manifesting as passivity or waiting to be told what to do.

- Imbalanced relationships where labor is unequally distributed, and you expect others to take care of you.

- Susceptibility to groupthink, and an automatic conformity with the prevailing opinion. Independence of mind is unavailable, and feels dangerous.

INDULGER AND RESTRICTOR (SPENDER AND SAVER)

Integrating Indulger and Restrictor allows you to Balance:

- Immediate gratification **and** deferred gratification
- Spending **and** saving
- Appetite **and** Sufficiency
- Enjoying the present **and** considering the future

THE INDULGER (SPENDER)

Indulger is the part of each of us which seeks immediate pleasure from indulging desire.

How Indulger Protects You

Indulger is the part of you which allows you to give yourself what you desire. This part prioritizes your immediate needs and wants, and provides the impetus to go after them. It protects you from feeling left out and deprived.

This character is a seeker of pleasure, the part that scratches an itch. It will keep you from missing out on life's rich buffet of experiences. It narrows focus to what you want right now, often to the exclusion of longer-term desires.

The Indulger is the master of substitution: it will focus your attention on an immediate need as a way of keeping you distracted from deeper needs. It's far easier, after all, to lust after the latest gadget than to confront a deeper desire for belonging or meaning. Like its close cousin the Comfort Seeker, Indulger is a big fan of numbing out, indulging yourself as a way of not feeling difficult emotions.

The Indulger Insider

When you feel powerless to resist a temptation, you can be pretty sure your Indulger is activated. It doesn't create desires as much as magnify them, until they feel irresistible.

The Indulger Insider often emerges as a larger-than-life persona, the gourmand who's hungry to taste and savor all that life has to offer. Desires present themselves with such force that it can feel near impossible to deny yourself, or even to delay. The Indulger Insider sees little point in delayed gratification. Why wait, when you can have what you want right now?

There is often a marked fear of missing out (FOMO), an anxiety that if you don't get what you want right now, it will be gone, and will never return. Paradoxically, this character is both the most likely to over-indulge, and the most likely to experience a feeling of scarcity. The more you indulge, the more you can keep at bay the feeling that there won't be enough for you, that your needs will never be met.

The Indulger Insider is particularly prone to falling into addictive patterns, with any substance or experience that lights up the brain's pleasure centers. This can take many forms, from the chocoholic who continues to munch when not hungry, to the shopaholic with a closet full of outfits they have little opportunity to wear. In both cases, the short-term pleasure overwhelms longer-term considerations (your waistline, or your financial health).

The Indulger Insider is particularly susceptible to suggestion. The moment you see someone else who has something nice, you find yourself wanting it too.

Origins of the Indulger

Indulger is a response to scarcity, to the fear that there won't be enough for you. The Indulger tends to emerge in people who experienced scarce resources of all kinds, from food to money, from opportunity to attention.

The Indulger can emerge as a reaction to restriction, or the expectation of future restriction. For example, if you were brought up in a diet culture that advocated restricting certain foods, the Indulger will emerge to ensure you grab them (and over-consume them) while they are available, before the restrictions inevitably clamp down again.

When the Indulger is activated on your Inner Team without the balancing influence of the Restrictor, you may experience:

- Overindulgence, to the point of bingeing and gluttony.
- Difficulty deferring short-term desires in favor of long term needs (i.e. spending now vs saving for later).
- Difficulty with moderation, knowing how much is enough.

THE RESTRICTOR
The Restrictor is the part of each of us which limits and restricts the choices we can make.

How the Restrictor Protects You

The Restrictor determines what is permitted, and what is off-limits. It's the Restrictor that tells you not to eat empty calories or spend money on frivolities. This is the part of you which can keep candy in the cupboard without being tempted to eat it.

The Restrictor can help you hold onto extra money without it burning a hole in your pocket. It can turn down dessert without feeling deprived.

The Restrictor protects your future. While it may appear to be denying you pleasure, the Restrictor is protecting you by focusing you on longer-term objectives. It's largely uninterested in the present, and directs your attention away from passing desires and fancies towards the bigger, longer-term goals of the future. It's the part of you that advocates reducing your spending now to save for retirement later.

The Restrictor can resemble the Judge. Rather than exercising moral judgments, however, its judgments are applied to food, money and pleasure. Like the Judge, the Restrictor offers a kind of clarity about good and bad which allows you to make choices.

The Restrictor Insider

The Restrictor Insider is exceptional at setting and holding boundaries about your own behavior. From the outside, people with a Restrictor Insider appear to be extraordinarily disciplined. The Restrictor's true superpower, however, isn't discipline but the capacity to defer gratification.

When the Restrictor is an Insider, your identity begins to be linked to your choices when faced with temptations. It divides the world into good and bad choices, healthy and unhealthy options, and is insistent that you make wise choices now in order to support your thriving in future. If you've ever felt virtuous because, for example, you choose to not eat meat, or you eat only organic food, this is a sign that your Restrictor could be an Insider on your Inner Team.

You will find the Restrictor's signature in the beliefs of diet culture. It's the source of advice that restricting what you eat is the pathway to health, and the accompanying judgment that those who can do this are somehow morally superior to those who can't. What the Restrictor doesn't grasp is that the more you restrict a particular food or experience, the more attractive it becomes. At the extreme, the Restrictor Insider can be rather ascetic, believing that the desire for pleasure is something to distrust.

Origins of the Restrictor
The Restrictor is modeled and reinforced by the way our culture talks about both food and money. There are entire industries (diet, financial planning) that have repeated Restrictor messages so often, they've become conventional wisdom. This "wisdom" is often passed on by parents to their children, and from experts to the uninformed, who internalize the Restrictor's guiding principles.

While the capacity to say no, operate by a budget and defer gratification are important skills, so is learning to spend money on yourself, on what you really value, as is learning to truly savor the food you eat. These kinds of messages are often completely missing in the early lives of those who develop a strong Restrictor.

Rather than becoming useful guidelines that promote physical or financial well-being, the Restrictor's rules are the criteria we use to make judgments of ourselves and others.

When the Restrictor is operating on your Inner Team without the balancing influence of the Indulger, you may experience:

- Denying your present-day needs and wants, refusing to spend money on yourself.

- Rigidity and inflexibility about your food choices, or your budget.
- Habitually self-denying, to the point where you lose touch with your desire
- Living in the future, to the point that you suffer or feel deprived in the present

JUDGE AND NEUTRAL

Integrating Judge and Neutral allows you to Balance

- Forming opinions **and** keeping an open mind
- Concluding **and** rethinking
- Enforcing definitive principles **and** embracing multiple paths

NOTE: Judging the Judge

A pause is needed before you dive into the profile of the Judge. Judge is one of the harder characters to see appreciatively. Or to put it another way, you probably judge your Judge, believing that it's far better to be non-judging than judgmental.

Ironically, this opinion – that judging is bad and non-judgment is good – is exactly the kind of decision your Judge makes.

Whether you're conscious of it or not, the Judge is involved in every opinion you form, and every decision you make. Becoming conscious of it opens the door for judgment to become a constructive rather than destructive force in your life. It's the difference between having good judgment, and being judgmental.

When you think of a judgmental person, you're likely to bring to mind someone who is critical. But approving of someone is a judgment too. The Judge informs who and what you praise, as much as who and what you make wrong. Whether approving or disapproving, the Judge's role is to differentiate and discern. Its questions are evaluative, designed to push you towards taking a position and forming an opinion: Is this good or bad? Acceptable or unacceptable? Ethical or unethical?

Without the Judge, Communities and societies would not be able to establish or adhere to stable laws or norms. Individually, you would be lost, unable to navigate in society, deprived of the capacity to form opinions and make choices. It's the Judge who establishes in-group and out-group boundaries, the foundation of our sense of belonging.

As you read the descriptions that follow, try pausing your judgment of your Judge. Get curious about how it protects you, and what its superpower – discernment – makes possible in your life. Notice its action as you evaluate and make meaning of what you're experiencing.

You may just find that becoming aware of the reach and influence of your Judge, and learning how to partner with it constructively, is one of the most important pieces of personal development work you will ever do.

THE JUDGE
The Judge is the part of each of us which discerns, differentiates and evaluates, allowing you to form opinions and make choices.

How the Judge Protects You
The Judge is the part of you that already knows enough to form an opinion. Its mind is made up. It's the "decider" of your Inner Team.

The Judge protects you by drawing clear lines between good and bad, permitted and forbidden, acceptable and unacceptable. It warns against behaviors that would expose you to negative judgments from other people, and encourages behaviors designed to earn their positive judgments.

The Judge attempts to create a feeling of belonging through affinity with those who share your judgments, operating by the assumption that *the enemy of my enemy is my friend.* Brene Brown has termed this "common enemy intimacy". It's an example of how the Judge is attuned to consensual principles that hold groups together, creating an "us" to belong to, and a "them" to react against.

Internally, the Judge guards you against feeling vulnerable through the mechanism of projection. Rather than identifying faults, flaws or deficiencies in yourself, it directs your attention outwards to discover these in other people. The Judge itself is often projected, which you may experience as the feeling that everyone around you is judging you.

The Judge Insider

Because the Judge is archetypal and present in everyone, it's an Insider by default.

A Judge Insider generates the feeling of certainty that you're right, and that others are wrong (or vice versa). Whether you're certain you're right about your political opinions, the best type of beer to drink, or the right way to raise a child, your Judge is pulling the strings.

The Judge isn't burdened by doubt, and is deeply suspicious of neutrality. It divides the world into us and them, right and wrong, in order to keep you in the us/right camp. A Judge Insider simplifies the world, rejecting complexity in favor of the opinion that the right things to do are obvious to right-thinking people (like you). Anyone who doesn't agree simply doesn't "get it". For the Judge, the only purpose of debate is to win others over to your side of an argument (the right side, obvs). The Judge Insider generates outrage, and its close cousin, self-righteousness. It both causes and thrives in the polarized world of politics, and the social media echo chambers which reinforce it.

The Judge operates by one foundational assumption: <u>you already have all the information you need</u>. This has the effect of shutting down curiosity about learning more. Any time you think an answer is obvious, your Judge has convinced you it's unnecessary to ask any further questions. The Judge knows, for sure, what's right and wrong, and wants you to make up your mind even when you're missing crucial information (otherwise known as prejudice, literally "pre-judging"). For the Judge, the desire to settle on a solution crowds out curiosity about the problem.

The Judge can operate as a kind of "reality police", dismissing evidence that contradicts what it has decided is true. For the Judge, if evidence contradicts my beliefs, the evidence must be false. For example, think of a physician dismissing the benefits of complementary healing modalities without examining the evidence, or a person of faith dismissing the insights of science.

You'll notice your Judge at work when you form an overwhelmingly strong first impression of someone, either positive or negative. It's pulling your strings when you reach a snap decision with limited information.

The Judge appears to take an attacking posture, but it's fundamentally defensive. The Judge defends the "rightness" of how you understand the world against anything and anyone that would threaten it. The Judge Insider displays closed-mindedness, often proudly.

The Judge likes to label, and then sees the label, not the person. For example, there's a world of difference between calling someone a drunk (labeling), and being aware that they sometimes drink to excess (discerning).

The Judge is characterized by the feeling that you are entitled – even *required* - to make moral assessments of others. The moral rating system is always tilted in favor of what you designate as right, proper, and appropriate.

When the Judge is activated, curiosity and empathy are crowded out. For example, listen to a radio talk show or podcast which advocates any strong ideological position. You'll hear the Judge berating anyone who believes something different, without curiosity about why they might believe what they believe. The Judge crowds out exploration of differences, producing thinking which is evaluative and fixed, rather than exploratory and open.

In relationships, the Judge Insider can struggle to maintain connection when differences emerge. The Judge knows what's right, and wants to be in relationship with those who are also right. The Judge will be reluctant to permit a close, trusting relationship with someone it has judged as wrong.

How the Judge Partners with Other Characters
If you pay close attention to the content Judge's opinions, evaluations and judgments, you'll see evidence of other Insiders on the Inner Team. Positive judgments reflect the values of the Insiders, negative judgments reflect the values of the Outsiders.

Here are a couple of everyday examples:

- You feel irritated when you see another driver make a turn without signaling.
  - o The Judge activates to reinforce that rule breaking is bad, reinforcing a Rule Follower Insider, and a Rebel Outsider
- You admire one sibling's selflessness in caring for your elderly

parent, and feel resentful towards another sibling's apparent disinterest, which you label as selfish.

o The Judge is reinforcing the rule that you should think of others before yourself, suggesting a Pleaser Insider, and Boundaried Outsider.

The Judge will see your Outsiders in others rather than in yourself. The more you have disowned a particular character in yourself, the greater the intensity of your judgment of others will be.

The Judge and the Inner Critic

The Judge is often confused with the Inner Critic, because both use judgment as a primary tool. The difference is that the Judge focuses attention externally, seeing flaws in others, whereas the Critic focuses inwardly, seeing flaws in oneself. It's the same judgmental attack, applied to a different target. The Judge's position asserts your superiority compared to others; the Critic's position affirms your inferiority.

The Origins of the Judge

When self-esteem is low, the Judge can emerge to replace this with a feeling of superiority of being better than *those people*.

You may have grown up in an environment where the adults frequently passed judgment, modeling this behavior. The judgments may have reflected a religion's strict moral codes, a political ideology or a strong cultural preference.

You may have experienced schools or peer groups which were exclusionary rather than inclusive, and learned to adopt the same judgments to fit in.

Social media posts that are designed to generate outrage

are examples of the Judge at work, and these can normalize (and even celebrate) a judgmental way of being in the world.

Growing up in a monoculture is also a factor in the development of the Judge. A lack of exposure to differences slows the development of the empathy that is necessary to relate non-judgmentally to otherness.

If the Judge is operating on your Inner Team without the balancing influence of Neutral, you may experience:

- Closed-mindedness, stubbornly adhering to what you believe to be true without curiosity about other points of view.

- A tendency to attach negative labels to other people.

- Difficulty forming relationships with people who do not share your opinions

- Feeling an irresistible urge to correct others, from their grammar to their life choices.

NEUTRAL
Neutral is the part of each of us which refuses to take sides, remains neutral and reserves judgment.

How Neutral protects you
Neutral protects you from the risks associated with taking sides, such as being trapped in a position from which you cannot escape. It operates from the principle that safety comes from hedging your bets and keeping your options open.

Neutral offers the protection of adaptability. Because no opinion is permanent and no position is carved in stone, changing your mind or adjusting your opinion costs far less than if you had declared your final answer. The permission to change your mind allows you to respond to changing circumstances rapidly and fluently.

The signature mental state of this character is openness. It allows you to be open to influence, to take in new information, to reconsider a previous opinion. In a polarized world, Neutral is an independent.

The Neutral Insider

The Judge operates from the assumption that it already has enough information to form an opinion; Neutral does not see a need to form an opinion in the first place. This character will not be pressed into drawing premature conclusions (pre-judging). On the rare occasions when the Neutral Insider offers an opinion, it will be stated tentatively rather than definitively.

This character's capacity to remain open makes the Neutral Insider a natural mediator. Perspective taking – seeing an issue from multiple points of view - comes effortlessly: it's as much a reflex for Neutral to walk in someone else's shoes as it is for Judge to evaluate. Feeling no pressure to privilege one point of view over another, this character is an enormous asset when you're encountering diversity and complexity. It is comfortable with paradox and contradiction.

Neutral Insiders have a distinctive way of relating. This character can be easygoing, flexible and adaptable, but also vague and hard to pin down. This can frustrate people who want to know where you stand, who want to know where your boundaries are. This reaction can be particularly intense from a person who has a Judge Insider, for whom relationship is conditional on knowing whether you're with them or against them.

Neutral is actively reinforced in many professions. For example, in the sciences, this position of remaining open as you gather data is crucial. The fields that attempt to make sense of the complexity and diversity of humans, from psychology to social work to education, also demand the capacity to withhold judgment.

Origins of Neutral

When giving the wrong answer might subject you to criticism or judgment, giving no answer at all is an effective way to stay safe. It can emerge as a response to certain types of conflict in your early environment, such as feeling pressured to take sides between arguing parents.

Whatever the specific circumstances, Neutral emerges as a response to the need to make sense of differences. Growing up in a highly diverse, multicultural environment will do this.

When Neutral is present on your Inner Team without the balancing Influence of the Judge, you may experience:

Your reluctance to form an opinion or take a position can lead to you being perceived as a fence sitter, slippery, evasive or even disengaged.

- Your reluctance to form stable conclusions can set in motion a pattern of endlessly gathering information without generating knowledge, or reaching firm conclusions.

- An unwillingness to set boundaries based on stable ethical and moral principles.

- You can overuse your capacity to adapt and flex yourself, to the point where you lose contact with what you believe and stand for.

LOYALIST AND FREE AGENT

Integrating Loyalist and Free Agent allows you to balance:

- Steady commitment **and** opportunism
- Keeping your word **and** changing your mind
- Resisting endings **and** embracing beginnings

THE LOYALIST

The Loyalist is the committed part of each of us which values loyalty, tenacity and grit.

How the Loyalist Protects You

The Loyalist is the most tenacious character on the Inner Team. It protects by providing the energy to keep going when it would be easier to walk away. It can summon the determination to push through difficult tasks, persevere in adverse conditions, and never give up.

Loyalist protects against the fear of the unknown by its choice to be loyal to what is already familiar, whether a relationship, a job, or even a preferred brand. It operates by a philosophy of "better the devil you know."

Loyalist serves as a buffer against loss and grief that arise when you leave a job or end a relationship. If you never leave, you never have to feel those particularly poignant emotions.

The Loyalist brings steadiness, dependability and consistency to relationships. Above everything, Loyalist strives to make you worthy of trust, as a person who is in it for the long haul.

When Loyalist is an Insider

The Loyalist is celebrated in US culture with maxims like, "Winners never quit, and quitters never win." The Loyalist Insider can be very judgmental about those who quit when things get hard, those who walk away from commitments. It interprets endings almost as moral failures. The worst insult you could offer the Loyalist is "quitter". As a result, the Loyalist will not allow you to even contemplate leaving a bad job or an unhappy marriage. Struggle and suffering are embraced as an inevitable part of life, and your worth is tied directly to your capacity to withstand it. A willingness to suffer is often displayed as a badge of honor.

Loyalty for this character can take many forms. Loyalty in a relationship or to family are highly prized, as is loyalty to an employer. This character can show up as a "company man" who will steadily work year after year in service of an organization's mission. The Loyalist Insider values tenure. Showing up consistently over time is a source of pride.

It can show up in the form of lifelong, unswerving devotion. This can be focused on anything, from a sports team to a philanthropic cause. The Loyalist-powered sports fan, for example, will have you support your chosen team even through losing seasons, while looking disdainfully at fair-weather fans and bandwagon-jumpers. Whatever the team, cause or relationship, the Loyalist intends to stay committed for life.

Loyalists will remain loyal to brands and products, from cars to restaurants. There is a marked reluctance to change allegiances of any sort. The Loyalist will even be loyal to things: they'll work harder than any other type to fix a broken appliance, for example, not necessarily out of frugality, but because they refuse to walk away.

Overused, the virtue of loyalty can cross over into bloody-minded stubbornness. It's an overused Loyalist that will be most critical of flip-flopping, interpreting changing your mind as a moral failing.

Origins of the Loyalist
The Loyalist tends to become an Insider for those who have experienced abandonment or betrayal. The Loyalist ensures that you will never inflict the pain of abandonment on anyone else. Loyalist serves as a stable inner parent to the abandoned child within.

Sometimes, the Loyalist emerges as a response to being punished or humiliated for breaking a commitment or changing your mind.

Whatever the origins of your Loyalist, it will serve you by keeping your life more stable and consistent, cementing the bonds that connect you to other people and your community.

When Loyalist operates in your Inner Team without the balancing impact of the Free Agent, you may experience:

- Tolerating a failing relationship, job, or home for too long, prolonging suffering.

- Difficulty letting go and initiating endings, to avoid the feelings of loss and grief

- Stubbornness

- A marked resistance to change

- Susceptibility to the sunk cost fallacy: continuing to try and make something work because of the effort and money already invested, even when it's clearly failed.

THE FREE AGENT
The Free Agent is the part of each of us which desires freedom, above all else.

How the Free Agent Protects You
The Free Agent is the part of you which pushes against constraint, and refuses to be pinned down. It's the part of you which prefers to keep your options open, to avoid fixed commitments. It develops as a response to the fear of being trapped, without agency or choice.

Free Agent is the part of you that can help you embrace the necessity of endings, and deal with the grief they engender. It brings the courage to leave the known and familiar, and step into the unknown. Whether leaving a job, ending a relationship, moving to a new city, or choosing to consciously renegotiate a prior commitment, this character is a powerful protector of your liberty and choice.

Free Agent as an Insider
The Free Agent has an unusual superpower: the ability to not only see multiple options, but to see each as a viable choice. It does not feel constrained by history, nor swayed by convention. If offered a choice of going through door number one and door number two, Free Agent will immediately look for door number three to escape through. For this reason, those with a strong Free Agent character on their Inner Team are often perceived as being highly innovative. While this may be true, the Free Agent's core motivation isn't to bring something new into the world, but to experience yourself as free to choose.

The Free Agent never considers <u>any</u> decision to be final and irrevocable. If there was a phrase that captures the essence of

this character, it's *"...for now."* As in, "I'll take the job... for now."
The Free Agent is not commitment-phobic as much as it's free-
dom-seeking. The Free Agent will seek freedom within commitments, liking the sense of freedom that comes with a job and a
side hustle, or an open marriage.

The Free Agent can produce behaviors that are quite mercenary. This is the part of you that will make temporary commitments to the highest bidder, and finds the concept of loyalty to be
quaintly anachronistic. The mercenary Free Agent can be seen in
athletes who change teams to play for rivals; businesspeople who
jump to a competitor who offers a better salary; the gig worker
or consultant who constantly jumps from project to project. The
Free Agent's mercenary tendencies can also be seen in people
who "play the field" sexually, jumping from partner to partner
without ever committing. The mercenary is a highly self-protective form of the Free Agent, keeping you from getting trapped in
situations where you are exploited or taken for granted.

Free Agent can also show up as a social butterfly. This is the
flighty part of you that isn't satisfied by being a part of a single friend group or social circle, but switches rapidly between
multiple groups. The gift of this flighty character is living in the
present, being able to recognize and respond to shifting desires,
operating with freedom.

Free Agent can look indecisive from the outside, but that
doesn't quite capture the essence of the character. It's not so
much an unwillingness to make decisions, as a pattern of making many decisions and then changing them again when needed.
At the extreme, this character can become maddeningly unreliable, a crazymaking influence in relationships where there is an
expectation of consistency.

Origins of Free Agent

When Free Agent comes to prominence in your Inner Team, there is often some early experience of feeling trapped or over-controlled.

Sometimes, there's a history of failed relationships, and an unconscious expectation that you will be abandoned or rejected. Free Agent offers the solution that it's less painful if you're the one doing the rejecting.

Whatever your unique story, your Free Agent character protects you against the vulnerability inherent in facing difficult challenges, the fear that you might not have what it takes to succeed.

When Free Agent operates in your Inner Team without the balancing impact of the Loyalist, you may experience:

- Commitment claustrophobia.

- A habit of reopening and re-examining decisions that have already been made.

- A tendency to confuse and disorient others by your frequent changes in direction, priority, or decision.

- A tendency to walk away rather than work through problems; for example, in a troubled marriage, a house in need of major repairs, a pet who needs extra training to be a good companion.

MATERIAL AND SPIRITUAL

Integrating Material and Spiritual allows you to balance:

- Empirical knowing **and** Intuitive knowing
- Skepticism **and** Faith
- Measurable **and** ineffable
- The knowable **and** the mysterious

MATERIAL

Material is the part of each of us who trusts only what can be seen, touched, measured or known through the five senses.

How it Protects You

Material helps you achieve a sense of security by focusing only on what you can know, for sure, to be objectively, demonstrably true. Material will ignore or minimize any aspect of human experience which does not fit this definition, making the world feel more understandable and less mysterious.

When Material is an Insider

The Material character is the most concrete and literal character on the Inner Team. Its focus is on what can be known through the five senses, what can be objectively measured. Operating as an Insider, it is not so much materialistic as unsure what to make of anything non-material, abstract or intangible. This character is typically uninterested in concepts like meaning, fulfillment, purpose or mission, preferring what is real, undeniable, provable.

Material has the capacity to tune out noise and identify signal, to cleave to facts and to set aside stories. This character typically demonstrates a strong preference for non-fiction, and may believe that fiction is rather pointless. Metaphors and analogies are seen as distorting reality, and are distrusted. Material prefers directness and specificity: say what you mean and mean what you say.

The Material Insider seeks certainty, and finds it in quantitative questions such as *how much, how often, how many, how far.* It's this character that likes to quantify life, and has an affinity for technologies such as fitness trackers, budget trackers, and similar.

When operating in partnership with Rational, this character has the superpower of dispassionate observation of reality, and can achieve a high level of objectivity. It's particularly well-adapted to work in the physical sciences, engineering, accounting, or similar fields that deal with the concrete, knowable, and measurable. In the arts, and to a lesser degree the social sciences, the Material character struggles to find what is true and can be trusted, and distinguish it from what is invented.

At the extreme, the Material character can become dismissive of anything that does not fit its concrete, quantitative schema. This is particularly pronounced when Material is operating in tandem with the Judge. Anything in the domain of spiritual experience, faith, or religion is rejected as making no sense at all. The term "pseudo-science" or "nonsense" is commonly used to disparage anything that doesn't fit the scientific, materialistic world.

In the professional realm, this same judgment privileges "hard skills" over "soft skills," not so subtly diminishing the value of the latter. Material likes to divide the world into real work and false work, in which real is what is concrete and measurable (finances, market share, growth rates, etc.), and false work (referred to as fluff) is anything in the domain of emotion and the human spirit, like employee engagement, culture, mission or purpose.

The Material Insider focuses on parts not wholes. Anything in nature can be understood by looking at its component parts. This character is excellent at reductionist thinking, but struggles with systems thinking, on connections between parts. As an example, someone with a strong Material character would likely focus narrowly on a single data point such as one's carbon footprint, rather than trying to understand the interactions between the many human and natural ecosystems that impact our climate.

Origins of Material

Frequently, those with a strong Material character grew up in households that experienced poverty. Acquiring material possessions became the strategy to never again experience the fear of not having enough.

This character can also emerge as a rebellion against an environment that placed the spiritual and religious over the worldly. Think of a child of a free spirit who grows up to be a banker. Conversely, it can emerge as a strategy to fit in within a militantly atheist home.

When Material is operating in your Inner Team without the balancing influence of Spiritual, you may experience:

- Difficulty in articulating a vision for one's life that extends beyond financial security.

- Certainty about what is true and what is not, leading to closed-mindedness.

- Taking on the role of "reality police," dismissing anything that doesn't fit a hard scientific schema (sometimes referred to as scientific fundamentalism).

- A preference for things over people (e.g. the car makes sense, people do not).

- Greed, in the sense of acquiring or consuming *more* than you need, accompanied by the feeling that no matter how much you have, it's never enough. Trying to fill a sense of inner emptiness with things (toys, possessions, wealth, etc.)

SPIRITUAL
Spiritual is the part of each of us which is connected to the non-physical, intangible world of faith, intuition and energy.

How Spiritual Protects You
Spiritual creates a feeling of unity, of connection with all things. It's a balm to a feeling of separateness or isolation. Spiritual can sense a higher purpose, something beyond personal desires and needs. It finds the transcendent within the mundane, living in a world that is alive, vital and imbued with meaning.

Spiritual relieves the mind of sole decision-making responsibility by being open to guidance. There is a sense of safety and inner rightness when you sense that your actions are being guided by a higher power.

Spiritual is drawn to the idea of transcendence. It believes that it's possible to rise above your struggles and pain, and elevate your consciousness beyond worldly concerns. This is a double-edged sword. It's a source of a higher perspective on what is occurring in your life, and a form of emotional armor, attempting (usually unsuccessfully) to meditate or pray away the messy, painful work of healing.

When Spiritual is an Insider

The Spiritual character focuses your attention on the non-physical, non-measurable aspects of human experience. It is the part of you that sees the world as fundamentally mysterious, no matter how much you think you know about it. To Spiritual, there is always a deeper reality than can be observed with the five senses. This is captured by Helen Keller's famous quote: "The best and most beautiful things in the world cannot be seen or even touched, they must be felt with the heart."

Spiritual has an unquenchable curiosity about the invisible world, and how everything is connected to everything else. Its language tends to be poetic, metaphoric, and evocative. Spiritual sees the heart and subtler senses as a more reliable source of information than the five senses. What is emotionally resonant is seen as true. Scientific thinking is not dismissed, per se, but seen as incomplete. Intuition can see what the analytic mind cannot: love, faith, unity/connectedness, the vital energy that animates all life.

When Spiritual is an Insider on the Inner Team, your identity will reflect your sense of connection with nature and the divine. Your material reality – where you live, your physical body, your possessions – does not define you.

Spiritual is often found working in close partnership with another character. For example, when operating in partnership with the Rule Follower, Spiritual can show up as super devout, demonstrating a kind of "holier than thou" piety. Spiritual partnering with Judge criticizes people who are "not spiritual enough". When operating in partnership with the Perfectionist, Spiritual can create pressure to be enlightened, judging materialistic desires as moral failings. Spiritual partnering with Special produces a kind of glamorous spirituality, in which one's spiritual awareness, intuition and sensitivity are displayed, and earthy practicality or money-mindedness are seen as shameful and kept hidden.

Origins of Spiritual

Many people with a strong Spiritual character trace its origins back to a powerful experience that cannot be understood without a spiritual perspective. These can include experiences like premonition, communication across time or distance, a miracle, or a felt sense of our unity with all beings and with nature. Unexplainable phenomena seem to activate this character to make sense of our experiences of this unseen, intangible world.

Alternatively, Spiritual can come to prominence on the Inner Team as a response to a perception of the emptiness of materialistic pursuits. The capitalist ethos of growth and acquisition is seen as a race to nowhere, a competition that has enormous costs for individuals, communities and the planet.

Whatever its origin in your early life, Spiritual offers the experience of a world full of aliveness and hidden possibility, in which the unknown is a mystery to explore rather than a threat.

When Spiritual is operating in your Inner Team without the balancing influence of Material, you may experience:

- Disengagement from the everyday world, disinterest in material concerns such as managing money, being aware of time.

- Difficulty accepting and integrating one's own materialism (e.g. a charismatic minister who preaches spiritual principles, but secretly amasses a large fortune).

- Distrust of evidence when it conflicts with what feels intuitively right (leading to a susceptibility to confirmation bias).

MINIMIZER AND MAXIMIZER

Integrating Maximizer and Minimizer allows you to balance:

- Over-reacting **and** Under-reacting
- Drama **and** peace
- Expanding yourself **and** shrinking yourself

THE MINIMIZER

The Minimizer is the part of each of us which downplays importance and urgency.

How the Minimizer Protects You

The Minimizer is a strategy to cope with challenging circumstances. Rather than feeling the fear that you might not be equipped to meet the challenge, the minimizer reduces it to a level you can handle. This protective strategy is designed to keep you functioning in stressful situations.

Since it's hard to think clearly when flooded with intense feelings, the Minimizer's capacity to temporarily soothe anxiety makes space for other characters to bring their gifts to bear. For example, Minimizer can create a clearing for Rational to coolly analyze what's going on, or for Planner to design a course of action.

The Minimizer Insider

The Minimizer Insider turns mountains into molehills. If it had a catchphrase, it would be "It's no big deal." This response can be so instantaneous that genuine threats and problems can be ignored, set aside to be dealt with at a later date, or treated with a casualness that is out of proportion to the high stakes involved.

While it's tempting to conclude that the Minimizer distorts reality by pretending that big problems are really no big deal, this misapprehends what it's trying to do. The ability to adjust your perspective, to zoom out from what's happening in the moment to see it in a wider context, is this character's super-power. For example, when you're facing a challenging problem, the Minimizer will offer a perspective that it probably won't seem as important a month or a year from now. It can restore a sense of perspective.

The Minimizer Insider wants to smooth out the ups and downs of life. It supports your capacity to stay steady, calm and non-reactive. It makes it possible for you to surf waves of emotion rather than get tossed about by them.

One of the gifts of the Minimizer is a particular type of patience which allows the dust to settle before taking action. It embodies a "wisdom of delay", recognizing that many problems will solve themselves, if you can patiently allow events to play out.

The Minimizer tends to wear a mask of peaceful, positive calm, no matter what emotions may be roiling within. When it operates as an Insider, being calm can become an identity, making it genuinely hard to feel what is going on below the surface. In its more extreme presentations, this character can produce a kind of head-in-the-sand denial of reality. This can be particularly challenging in relationship, where meeting a minimizing reaction can leave others feeling unheard or even dismissed.

Origins of the Minimizer

People with particularly strong Minimizers sometimes describe having grown up with over-protective parents, who wanted to remove all difficulties and challenges from their child's life. You may have internalized their message that you're too sensitive to handle difficult experiences.

The Minimizer can also come to prominence when your early environment did not allow strong emotions. There are any number of external circumstances that could produce this, including family systems that were hyper-rational and uncomfortable with emotion generally.

It can also emerge when you have a sibling or other family member who demanded lots of attention. The Minimizer responds to this by minimizing your needs, raising the threshold beyond which you must say something.

If the Minimizer is operating on your Inner Team without the balancing influence of the Maximizer, you may experience:

- Dismissiveness and denial of anything you might find disturbing

- Complacency, under-reacting in the face of genuine threats

- Numbness, difficulty experiencing any emotion fully

- Passivity, waiting for change rather than initiating it

- A fixed facial expression, most commonly a bland smile to mask other feelings

THE MAXIMIZER
The Maximizer is the part of each of us which generates energy to respond rapidly to perceived threats and opportunities.

How Maximizer Protects You

It's tempting to stereotype the Maximizer as a kind of drama queen who catastrophizes every little challenge, but this misapprehends its protective role. This character demands and directs your attention to small issues, so you can prevent them from becoming big problems. It's a believer in the power of prevention and preparation.

The Maximizer enlarges and amplifies <u>everything</u>: your feelings, your needs, your opinions, your desires, your perceptions of the scale and urgency of your problems. It turns up the volume on what's happening inside you, so you notice it and can take action accordingly. The Maximizer doesn't particularly care what you <u>do</u> with the information: its job is simply to ensure that you've noticed it.

The Maximizer seems to have an amplifying effect on other Insiders. It makes any character's warnings that much harder to ignore. It seems to have a particular affinity for partnering with the Inner Critic: the Inner Critic will tell you what you're doing wrong, the Maximizer will catastrophize the impact of your error.

The Maximizer Insider

The Maximizer Insider turns molehills into mountains. It has the capacity to zoom in so close that something small looks very, very large.

This character is responsive to the kind of problems that others might overlook. For example, on the interpersonal level, it's the Maximizer who can pick up on micro-aggressions, or the subtlest hints of judgment. In the professional domain, this character can zoom in on an unexpected data finding from an experiment, an inconsistency in a policy, or a barely noticeable deviation from what was expected.

The superpower of the Maximizer is to confront reality. This character seems to be incapable of denial, believing that over-reaction is a safer strategy than under-reaction.

The Maximizer Insider is associated with interpersonal expressiveness. This character makes it challenging to conceal your reactions, because what you feel, you feel intensely. Where the Minimizer will often mask feelings, Maximizers do the opposite: they hide nothing. The Maximizer makes it near impossible to have a poker face, or to tell a lie without immediately giving it away.

The Maximizer Insider thrives on intensity, and often on drama. There is a preference for a high level of stimulation, and a taste for strong emotions. This character has a particular affinity for horror movies, rollercoasters, and risk-taking. Maximizers have been known to deliberately generate interpersonal conflict, just to make things interesting. Peace and stability create discomfort rather than relaxation for this character, which interprets them as a sign that the other proverbial shoe is about to drop.

Origins of the Maximizer
The Maximizer can emerge as a trauma response, in situations where the trauma could have been foreseen and possibly prevented. The Maximizer emerges to make sure that future early warning signs are not ignored.

It can also emerge as a strategy to get attention from parents who are minimizers and conflict avoiders, or in large families where quiet voices are not heard.

When the Maximizer is operating on your Inner Team without the balancing influence of the Minimizer, you may experience:

- Hair-trigger reactivity and rapid escalation of emotions: can go from calm to rage, for example, in a nanosecond.

- Hypochondriac tendencies: every symptom means you're dying

- Chicken-Little effect: the frequency of raising concerns can lead to Maximizers being tuned out.

- A tendency to use exaggerated language, such as *always, never, best, worst, perfect, disaster*

PARTICIPANT AND OBSERVER

Integrating Participant and Observer allows you to balance:
- Establishing connections **and** maintaining boundaries
- Sharing generously **and** conserving energy
- Joining in **and** watching from the sidelines

THE PARTICIPANT

The Participant is the part of each of us which wants to join in, engage with others and be part of society.

How the Participant Protects You

The Participant is the part of you which feels safest when you're with other people. It's the most actively social member of the Inner Team. This character's solution to loneliness is to move towards others, to be the one who takes the initiative to invite, welcome and host others.

Being with friends is more than just a pleasure or distraction for this character. Friendships and community are necessary nutrients. Togetherness is an almost spiritual experience, a reminder that while we have separate bodies, we are one in consciousness, our fates inextricably linked with each other.

The Participant Insider

When Participant is an Insider, your identity is strongly linked to the role you play in groups. When you are on your own, you may feel a bit adrift. When you are with others, you know who you are. Social connection is as essential to you as water and oxygen, and you reach out for it whenever you can. For you, there is no such thing as too much time with people you care about.

The Participant brings the desire and the need to build and sustain community, to contribute, to be part of something larger than yourself, to truly belong. You are acutely sensitive to any hint that you are being excluded, and you actively work to help others feel included, to know that they are valued and important.

You discovered early on that being the one to initiate connection was a better way to meet your needs than to wait to be invited. Your superpower is to be a welcoming host, a creator of spaces for people to connect. You intuitively grasp group dynamics, which informs your instincts about what to do to bring people closer.

In groups – whether friends, work colleagues or community – you feel a responsibility to participate actively and engage fully. You're often puzzled when people are reluctant to participate, as if their contribution didn't matter. And you're bemused by people who aspire to be independent and individualistic, when we're so obviously social creatures who need each other?

You bring presence, reciprocity and generosity into your relationships: show up, maintain an equal exchange, and be an active contributor. Following these principles, you are generous with your time, energy, attention and resources.

Origins of the Participant

Participant often emerges as a response to experiences of isolation, disconnection and loneliness. You found safety in your friendships and social groups, even when your parents or other adults in your life were neglectful or not present.

The development of the Participant is encouraged in families that are highly social. Perhaps your house was the gathering place for all the kids on your street, or the place where everyone in your family gathered at holidays. You likely got lots of modeling of social roles of being a host, and actively welcoming and including others.

When Participant operates on your Inner Team without the balancing influence of Observer, you may experience:

- A tendency to experience belonging and closeness by merging with the prevailing opinions of a group. Similarities are emphasized, differences are suppressed.

- May become over-extended socially, participating in so many groups that time alone is scarce.

- Operating from a desire for others to feel included, may interpret others' choice not to participate as a personal rejection.

THE OBSERVER
The Observer is the part of each of us which withdraws from engaging in social interactions, preferring the view from the sidelines.

How the Observer Protects You
The Observer helps you stay safely above the fray. When you watch from a distance rather than participating, you feel safer. When others get flustered and emotional, you are able to remain objective, calm and clear.

In particular, the Observer helps you stay in touch with yourself, and avoid being over-influenced by others. It creates space for you to know your own mind and heart.

The Observer Insider

The Observer Insider experiences a kind of claustrophobia from being too close to others, and strives to find a safer distance. You prize your ability to think clearly, observe dispassionately, and maintain objectivity about what you are seeing.

When you feel overstimulated socially, you'll check out. Sometimes this might involve physically leaving the room to find a space where you can hear yourself think. Sometimes you choose to stay in the room but mentally check out. Engaging with other people has a high energy cost for you, so much so that you may have wondered whether the benefits of being in relationship outweigh the costs. A calm, quiet mind and a private inner life feel more important and more nourishing to you than being in community.

The Observer Insider can be hesitant and socially cautious. There's an uncertainty about how to engage with other people: you're not sure quite what to say, when to say it, or if what you have to say will be welcomed. Not being certain quite how to engage, you often delay speaking up or offering an opinion. But by the time you are ready to speak, the moment to contribute has often passed. Over time, you have become accustomed to watching rather than participating, and it's become both a habit and a superpower, as you automatically gather and analyze information.

Origins of the Observer

Many people whose Inner Team has a strong Observer identify themselves as introverts. Whether or not, you may have a low threshold for overstimulation, sometimes from being very emotionally or energetically sensitive.

Like its close cousin, Boundaried, the Observer can emerge as a solution to an early environment in which you had little to no privacy, or where emotions were expressed at high volume.

When Observer is operating on your Inner Team without the balancing influence of Participant, you may experience:

- Isolation and loneliness

- A belief that relationships are an energy drain, sending a message of disinterest to other people.

- A pattern of hoarding your energy, withholding information, keeping secrets.

- Cynicism about belonging to organizations or groups (along the lines of Groucho Marx's famous statement, "I wouldn't want to be in any club that would have me as a member.")

PATRIARCH AND MATRIARCH

The Patriarch and Matriarch are archetypal characters who have a significant but often unseen impact. While they are rarely Insiders, both characters directly influence your beliefs and assumptions about gender, gender politics and the social roles of men and women. Unlike other pairs of characters in this book, this profile is not about balancing complementary opposites, but bringing both archetypes to conscious awareness.

THE PATRIARCH
The Patriarch internalizes the rules, assumptions and beliefs of a patriarchal society. It carries the belief that men and masculinity are superior to women and femininity.

The Patriarch reinforces conventional cultural beliefs about male and female roles, such as:

- "A man's job is to protect those he cares for, to provide for his wife and family"
- "Women should be at home raising children"
- "Men must always be strong, and never show weakness or show tender emotions."
- "Men must be tough, independent and never ask for help."

If any statement sounds chauvinistic, patronizing diminishing of women, or reinforcing male gender stereotypes, it may have originated with the Patriarch.

The Patriarch also holds negative beliefs about women:

- "Women are irrational, erratic, weak and in need of protection."
- "A strong woman who asserts power is not a real woman."
- "Women's power is sexual, and needs to be hidden because men will be powerless to resist it."

The Patriarch can be overtly prejudiced against women, but its influence is often covert. There is a default assumption that women, and traditional women's work are less valuable than men's. The Patriarch will categorize caring for children or the vulnerable as "not real work", leading to lower pay and lower respect. Its influence can be felt in attitudes to aspects of the workplace that touch on the traditionally female domains of emotions and relationships, degrading these as "touchy-feely" and "soft".

Even in individuals who are not overtly misogynistic, the Patriarch's beliefs and assumptions do not disappear. They continue to operate behind the scenes. Men can be involved in childrearing, for example, and women involved in traditionally male careers, but each may carry self-judgments about these roles, and be sensitive to the judgments of others. For example, if you've ever felt that being a successful professional woman makes you an inadequate mother, that's the Patriarch operating in tandem with the Inner Critic. Of course, if you were to focus on child-rearing to the exclusion of your professional goals, the Critic would criticize you for that too.

The Patriarch assumes the right to hold and use power, to take up space, to assert dominance (particularly over women, but also "beta male" men who are less alpha and more collaborative).

This character can be operating in the background of otherwise empowered women as a nagging guilt, confusion, or shame about claiming space, or exercising power and authority. It's the voice that says, "Let the man drive," or "Don't beat him in this game, it's better to let him win."

In overt patriarchy, men claim and hold power, adopting an authoritarian stance, and a sense of absolute entitlement to that privilege. But it is equally powerful when not conscious, operating as a hidden Insider, dominating thought patterns below the level of awareness. Hidden Insiders produce confusing behaviors: "I don't know why I keep doing that," or "I know it's okay to ask for help... I just don't do it."

The Patriarch's action in women can be seen in beliefs like, "I have to show I'm as tough as the men to get ahead," or "I can never let them see me express doubt." Archetypally feminine power, expressed through traditionally female roles such as nurturing and caring, is seen as less-than, a poor substitute for the "real thing". The Patriarch can also show up as a reflexive (and often fierce) criticism of women who do express masculine power.

For all the harm that the Patriarch causes to all genders, its intentions are protective. It advocates for order, stability, protection of those who cannot protect themselves. Even the belief that women should stay in the home has a protective intention, stemming from a (highly questionable) belief that if they were to enter the male world, they would be hurt.

The Patriarch works in tandem with the Protector to exert influence on which characters you are allowed to express in society. Men are permitted to express power characters, women are forbidden from doing so. The Patriarch also strongly affiliates with the Judge, to keep women and female power suppressed.

The Patriarch, out of balance with its opposite, looks a lot like toxic masculinity.

THE MATRIARCH

Just as the Patriarch represents archetypally male power, the Matriarch expresses archetypally female power. The Matriarch is proud of women, and not intimidated by men. The Matriarch cleaves to the idea that men may be physically stronger, but women are mentally and emotionally tougher, and far less fragile. She holds strong opinions about what it means to be a woman, daughter, mother, wife, sister, granddaughter and girlfriend, bringing to light the crucial importance and value of each role. The Matriarch assumes a position of primacy in a family system, operating from the foundational belief that no matter what the men may believe, it is the women who are really in charge.

Because the Matriarch operates in a patriarchal society, this character can become an Outsider on the Inner Team. When men and maleness are privileged, women and femaleness are relegated, diminished and unappreciated. Matriarch reverses this. Re-integrating this character, and giving her space to exert her influence, makes it possible for female power to be integrated and celebrated. Nurturing, caregiving, communicating and attending to emotion are returned to the center from the margins.

That said, the most common pattern associated with Matriarch and Patriarch is a power struggle, the battle of the sexes. Matriarch, after all, carries collective trauma and a deep resentment about thousands of years of male domination. This can manifest as a critical view of men: it is the Matriarch who will generate thoughts and statements like, "Men are responsible for the mess the world is in," or "If women were in charge, there'd be no wars." At the extreme, the Matriarch will pass judgment on all male traits, and take unerring aim at men's greatest vulnerabilities.

While this battle for power rages, an egalitarian relationship that is both intimate and peaceful will remain elusive. The solution requires an integration of maleness and femaleness, the capacity for both genders to be compassionate, caring and emotional and strong, assertive and rational.

PERFECTIONIST AND MESSY

Integrating Perfectionist and Messy allows you to balance:

- Tight/orderly **and** loose/unstructured
- Striving for better **and** knowing what's good enough
- Focusing on ideal state **and** embracing current state
- Attending to details **and** not sweating the small stuff

PERFECTIONIST

Perfectionist is the part of each of us which diligently strives to reach an ideal state of flawless excellence.

How Perfectionist Protects You

The Perfectionist protects you from being criticized. By setting the highest standards for your work, behavior and personal integrity, it attempts to place you safely beyond reproach.

For the perfectionist, the condition you must meet to be worthy is that you did your very best. It is the part of you that demands you get it right.

Perfectionist is the part of you which believes everything can be (and should be) improved. It will demand diligent and painstaking effort to achieve its vision, but it is a source of hope for a better future. It is this part of you that promotes the intuition that more is possible for you, that there is a better world just out of reach.

Perfectionist offers the safety of feeling that you are in control, that you can improve what you cannot tolerate.

Perfectionist as an Insider

The Perfectionist's superpower is discernment: the capacity to identify problems, defects and errors. It's this character who can spot something that is not in its proper place, from a picture hanging at an angle to an error in a spreadsheet. The perfectionist not only focuses your attention on problems, but connects your worth to your ability to fix them, to restore order.

For the Perfectionist, details matter. It's a powerful ally in situations where minor errors could have serious consequences, from performing surgery to conducting audits. It will not permit errors from carelessness, lack of preparation, or inattention to best practices.

The Perfectionist loves an efficient, smooth-running process. It will be incredulous, even offended when encountering unnecessary steps to accomplish a task. Wherever there is inefficient bureaucracy, there will be a Perfectionist who's desperate to fix it.

The Perfectionist is well-adapted to process improvement, less so to human development. Humans are not, after all, problems to be solved or processes to be perfected. No matter how much you may develop, mature and grow, you will remain forever imperfect, to the great consternation of the Perfectionist. The Perfectionist carries a core belief that everything can be made better by focusing on and correcting defects, but criticizing people into change has a poor track record.

The Perfectionist serves as a kind of curator in your life, determining what's okay to show the world, and what's not. This urge to present a perfected version of oneself to the world can manifest in many forms, including concealing errors, editing photographs of oneself to remove the tiniest imperfection, or being unwilling to ask for help.

Origins of the Perfectionist

The Perfectionist is one of the most common Insiders on the Inner Team, because it is an effective solution to a wide range of early challenges, and indeed to many of the challenges of adulthood too.

Common among these are being raised by critical parents, where being perfect was armor against their judgments. Many people with an active Perfectionist can describe experiences of having been shamed or humiliated for being spontaneous, disorganized, or messy.

It also emerges in environments where there is a great deal of attention paid to appearance, where the first commandment was to never make your parent(s) look bad.

You may have internalized the message that you were expected to have life all figured out, to not show that you're struggling, to appear perfectly put together. To show messiness, disorder or flaws was shameful.

When Perfectionist is functioning on your Inner Team without the balancing influence of Messy, you may experience:

- An overwhelming fear of failure, leading to avoidance of challenges that have a risk of failure, or which might trigger the feeling of not being good enough.

- A mental habit of finding fault, nitpicking small details, leading to a loss of perspective about the importance of relatively minor concerns (for example, someone who serves as the self-appointed grammar police)

- A defensive posture, where your attention is focused on guarding yourself against criticism.

- Expending disproportionate effort to achieve perfection, such as endless editing of a piece of writing.

- A tendency to over-research and over-analyze, unable to discern how much knowledge is enough.

- Setting high standards for others, and criticizing them for imperfections. In parenting and leadership, the recipient may internalize the message that they do not measure up.

- An unwillingness to compromise. Compromise is seen not as a method to help relationships by balancing one's needs with others', but as letting one's standards drop below what is acceptable.

MESSY (THE IMPERFECTIONIST)

Messy is the part of each of us which celebrates being forever imperfect, incomplete and beautifully flawed.

How Messy Protects You

Messy's protects you by helping you relax when you don't have control. It is the part of you that is radically accepting of what occurs in your life, particularly when you face the unexpected. It allows you to let go of any expectation of what *should* be happening, to loosen your grip. Rather than responding to the unknown with fear and contraction, this character will help you experience it as an adventure. If Messy had a slogan, it would be "Relax! Nothing is Under Control!"

Messy gives you permission to be human, to be perfectly imperfect. It offers the perspective that perfection doesn't exist, and wouldn't be desirable if it did. According to Messy, your flaws and imperfections humanize you and make you relatable.

Messy will support your ability to improvise and experiment

your way through the challenges you face, failing often without losing energy or enthusiasm.

Messy as an Insider

When Messy is an Insider on your Inner Team, you live your life without much of a plan, making it up as you go along. You don't expect order and predictability; quite the opposite. In direct contrast with the Perfectionist, who believes order is the natural state, Messy operates from the perspective that order is the exception, not the rule. For this reason, those with a strong Messy character thrive in disorder.

A Messy Insider often enjoys rocking the boat when things feel too orderly, tight or controlled. Messy can be a heretic, challenging assumptions, deliberately stirring things up. When Messy is an Insider, you are energized by the creative possibility of removing assumed constraints. You can be blissfully unaware of how crazymaking this can be for those who thrive on stability and have a high need for structure, who do not share your superpower of thriving in chaos.

Messy can be literally messy, leaving trails of papers or unwashed dishes wherever you go, and being thoroughly unbothered by wrinkled clothes or unbrushed hair. That said, there are plenty of outwardly tidy people who have a Messy Insider. Messy can express itself intellectually as an openness to new ideas, a willingness to challenge your assumptions. It can also express emotionally, as a willingness to get uncomfortable, enjoying the sensation of an unfamiliar emotion. It can even express spiritually, embracing a chaotic, disinterested universe in which meaning or purpose is endlessly unclear.

Messy does not expect tidy solutions and satisfying endings

where all loose ends are neatly tied up. You don't expect yourself to have it all figured out. You are comfortable not knowing. You expect to fail often, and are typically unbothered when this occurs. You will likely be drawn to professional roles where there's lots of change, and repelled from working in stable, mature systems which require nothing more than following the rules, which would feel stifling.

In relationship, Messy is highly permissive. You give yourself permission to be human, to not know, to experiment, and you offer this to others in kind. You're the opposite of rigid.

Origins of Messy

You may have faced an early environment in which the adults were hyper-critical of anyone or anything that didn't measure up to their high standards. The Messy character reflects a feeling that it's not possible to measure up, so why try? Its solution is to live in a way that's looser, more permissive and more accepting.

Whatever the specific origins of your Messy character, it will support your ability to live spontaneously, to free yourself from the pressure of trying to be perfect.

When Messy is operating on your Inner Team without the balancing influence of the Perfectionist, you may experience:

- A reluctance to set high standards for yourself or others, meaning that you can be over-tolerant of preventable errors.

- Overlooking the value of consistency.

- A tendency to lose track of everyday items (keys, wallet, etc.), because you put them down in random rather than consistent places.

PLANNER AND IMPROVISER

Integrating Planner and Improviser allows you to balance:
- Anticipating **and** responding
- Pre-determining your action **and** making it up as you go along
- Establishing order **and** embracing the unexpected

THE PLANNER
The Planner is the part of each of us which anticipates, prepares and organizes in order to influence future outcomes.

How the Planner Protects You
The Planner is a solution to the vulnerable feeling that you are out of control, being tossed around by fate, or that outcomes are predestined. It protects you with strategies to make the future feel more understandable, predictable and less overwhelming.

The Planner believes that safety comes from preparation. It's the boy scout of the Inner Team, operating by the mantra, "Be Prepared!" By directing your attention to the future, the Planner helps you prepare, so you're never blindsided or caught short.

This character considers multiple scenarios, a range of plausible outcomes, and creates a plan to respond appropriately to each. The feeling that you are ready for anything is a confidence booster, and a shield against the unexpected.

The Planner Insider
The Planner Insider seeks order. To leave anything to chance feels dangerous, as if you're courting disaster. Project plans,

spreadsheets, itineraries or task lists are not just useful, they feel like a survival necessity. Only when a plan is in place can you relax.

The Planner Insider lives in the future. It's the part of you which is focused less on what's happening right now, and more on what could or should happen in the future. This character is always thinking a few moves ahead, anticipating and preparing.

The Planner Insider is strongly associated with career success. The Planner's preference for taking charge of future outcomes is well adapted to the corporate world's "predict and control" approach to running a business. This works well in stable conditions where outcomes are relatively predictable, because the plan and the reality are likely to resemble each other. When facing novel, complex and volatile conditions, however, the Planner will often struggle, trying harder and harder to stay on plan, long after it was clear that adaptation was necessary. As a result, some people with a Planner Insider gravitate to work that is known and familiar, and avoid work that takes them into uncharted territories that are near impossible to plan for. For example, this character would prefer the orderliness of accounting to the unpredictability of crypto investing.

The Planner is a rather cerebral character, who thinks hard about how to achieve a desired outcome in future.

The Planner Insider is prone to over-preparation, for example by stockpiling supplies for every possible eventuality, packing clothes for every possible weather condition on a trip. A "plan B" feels like a security blanket.

The Planner's plans tend to be strongly influenced by other Insiders on the Inner Team. When operating in partnership with the Protector, which is constantly scanning for threats, plans will help you prepare for the worst-case scenario. When working with the Optimist, it will create a plan to capture emerging opportunities. When operating in partnership with Responsible, it will plan how you can always keep your word. When operating with the Perfectionist, you'll strive to achieve a perfect plan that covers all possible eventualities.

Origins of the Planner

The Planner emerges to bring order and predictability, often as a response to an early environment that was unpredictable, disordered or chaotic. Those with a Planner Insider often describe formative experiences of having been exposed to harm through being unprepared, and develop a strong Planner to ensure this never happens again.

When the Planner is operating on your Inner Team without the balancing Influence of Spontaneous, you may experience:

- A fantasy that a perfect plan is a reliable guard against all feelings of vulnerability. Frustration, disappointment or self-recrimination when reality doesn't conform to the details of the plan you made.

- A near-obsessional love of spreadsheets and project plans.

- Planning becomes an all-consuming mental activity, a form of armor. Rather than confront the vulnerable truth that life is unpredictable and uncontrollable, you plan as if it's possible to eliminate all threats, challenges or risks.

- Reluctance to look at the unstable foundations of a plan, recognizing how much it's based on unsubstantiated assumptions and educated guesses.

Differentiating The Planner and The Controller

The Planner and Controller are two characters which often show up in partnership on the Inner Team, but they have important differences. They are natural partners to each other, because planning is fundamentally an activity designed to achieve a feeling of being in control. The crucial distinction is that Planner is focused on achieving control of the future, whereas the Controller is focused on achieving control right now.

When they are activated on your Inner Team, however, they feel quite different. When Controller is present, you're likely to experience muscular tension, particularly a clenched jaw. A forward lean towards others is common. The Controller is a character that unapologetically takes up space.

The Planner is more cerebral. It's less present in the here and now, and more focused on what should happen in the future. Somatically, it's a more reserved energy, comfortable in the background, unlike Controller which has a preference for being front and center.

THE IMPROVISER

The Improviser is the part of each of us which responds in the moment, makes it up as you go along.

How the Improviser Protects You

Where Planner finds safety in a well-constructed plan, the Improviser finds safety in the freedom to respond in the moment. This character refuses to be controlled, pushing back against anything that will limit your freedom.

For many people, predictability is comforting. For the Improviser, the opposite is true: what is unpredictable is magnetically appealing, whether in people, places or experiences.

The Improviser Insider

The Improviser has little use for structure, and feels restricted by pre-determined responses. Consistency is stifling. Following a well-trodden path isn't just boring, it feels like the death of everything that makes life worth living.

This character demands and claims freedom, throws off any expectation that feels limiting, preferring to be unshackled by convention and habit. The Improviser is the part of you that wants to take a different route home every day, to try a different item on the menu every time you visit a restaurant. Variety is essential to this character.

Improviser doesn't see much value in planning and preparation. It will advocate being present and paying attention as a better strategy for responding to unpredictable demands and challenges. Those with an Improviser Insider will often thrive in situations where responses cannot be pre-planned. It will prefer speaking off the cuff rather than following a script, freewriting rather than following an outline, interpretive dance over detailed choreography. For the Improviser, life is a wild ride, an unscripted adventure. Conversations are improvisation, relationships a dance.

The Improviser is a close cousin to another low-structure character, Messy. They share a common capacity to accept what comes, to thrive in chaos, to enjoy the unpredictable. The distinction is that Messy is reacting against the demand to conceal all flaws and only do what you can do perfectly, whereas the Improviser is reacting against being controlled, particularly by plans that restrict freedom.

Origins of the Improviser

Those with a strong Improviser often describe an early environment where their survival was directly linked to the capacity to think on your feet, and respond rapidly to the unexpected. This is a character that develops when it's more important to be streetwise than book-smart.

When the Improviser is operating on your Inner Team without the balancing influence of the Planner, you may experience:

- A low boredom threshold: you can check out when there's not enough stimulation, or when you don't have free choice about how to respond.

- A tendency to re-invent the wheel: why use a tried a true solution, when you can have the fun of inventing (reinventing) a completely new way?

- Being unprepared, because it's more fun to figure out what to do when you don't have the right equipment than to do what's effective but predictable.

PLEASER AND BOUNDARIED

Integrating Pleaser and Boundaried allows you to balance:
- Heart **and** Backbone
- Your needs **and** my needs
- Saying yes (without feeling obligated) **and** Saying no (guilt-free)
- Warmth **and** strength

PLEASER
Pleaser is the part of each of us that wants to earn approval and inclusion by being of service to others' needs.

How Pleaser Protects You

By focusing your attention on pleasing other people, Pleaser protects you from being irrelevant, isolated and abandoned. The Pleaser generates a feeling that you are obliged to show up in a way that others will like and approve of.

The Pleaser's superpower of empathy helps you tune into what others feel, need and expect of you. Armed with this awareness, you adapt and accommodate yourself accordingly, and shapeshift into whomever they need you to be.

The Pleaser's focus on other people's needs is so intense and all-consuming that it can crowd out any awareness of your own needs. The Pleaser believes that attending to your own needs is selfish and unacceptable, because you are here for others, not for yourself.

The Pleaser Insider

When the Pleaser is an Insider on your Inner Team, people and relationships are your primary focus of attention. You try hard to be good. And for your Pleaser, being good means living in service to others, being self-sacrificing, generous, attentive, a giver not a taker. You will do anything to avoid being seen as selfish.

Your care for others' wellbeing is genuine, and inexhaustible. You are generous with your time and attention. You feel that you need to be needed. Your default answer to others' requests of you is "yes", although they may not need to ask, because you are so good at anticipating their needs.

You find saying "no" much, much harder to do, because it's difficult for you to bear their disappointment. When you do set a boundary, you may feel guilty, even walking back or apologizing for asking for what you need. When conflict occurs, your impulse is to back down, to appease and accommodate rather than holding your ground. You may find it hard to access anger as a way to defend your boundaries.

Your superpower to sense others' needs and expectations is unmatched. It doesn't matter whether you're tuning into a client, boss, partner or child, your empathy will reliably tell you who they need you to be, what will make them feel most cared for. You readily adapt yourself to become who they need.

Your sense of self-worth is inextricably linked to the emotions of the people in your life. When others are happy (and particularly, when they're happy *with you*), you feel great. When they're unhappy, it feels like a personal failure, and you feel worthless. When someone is unhappy with you, your impulse will be to redouble your efforts to fulfill their expectations, meet their needs, and alleviate their pain.

The Pleaser Insider is a natural accommodator. Flexing your-self to meet others' needs is so automatic that you barely notice you are doing it. Deferring or denying your own needs is equally automatic, to the point where you find it infinitely easier to name others' needs than your own. This enables you to work tirelessly for others, even if it requires depleting yourself. But when you feel the warmth of others' approval, it makes it all worthwhile.

The Pleaser's Origins

People with very active Pleasers often describe growing up alert for the signs of danger in another person's emotions. This could be a volatile, moody parent at home, or a bully at school. The Pleaser can also originate as a way to respond to the urgent demands of someone who was dependent on your care, such as a sick relative.

Whatever the specific circumstances, you internalized the message that others' needs are more important than your own. You may have been accused of "selfishness" if you did not auto-matically prioritize others over yourself.

You learned early on that saying "no" was dangerous. To do so was to risk judgment, anger and punishment. Saying yes to whatever was asked of you, from preparing a meal to cleaning up the house, was the solution that worked, the safer option. Saying yes kept the peace, sustained relationship. Your "yes" was the price you paid for inclusion. You began to believe that your purpose was to be of service, and the measure of your worth was whether others were pleased with you. When they weren't, you concluded that you were the cause, that you had not done enough.

If Pleaser is operating in your Inner Team without the balancing influence of Boundaried, you may experience:

- Saying yes automatically to what others ask of you (in the words of one ITD client: *"My yes button is stuck in an on position, and my no button doesn't work."*)
- Difficulty with knowing what you need, or prioritizing your needs over others'.
- Lack of connection with your own anger.
- A reluctance to take up space. Minimizing oneself, to avoid inconveniencing or being a burden on others.
- A reflex to back down when facing interpersonal conflict, and a deferential relationship with authority (or anyone on whom you feel dependent).
- A feeling that you are responsible for relieving others pain and suffering, prompting you to take on the role of rescuer (taking on others' problems as your own, offering unsolicited advice)
- Withholding your own ideas unless you're certain others will approve of them.
- Taking responsibility for ensuring that no one ever feels excluded or isolated.

BOUNDARIED
Boundaried is the part of each of us which attends to your own needs by setting and enforcing clear boundaries.

How Boundaried Protects You
Boundaried defends against the vulnerability of being taken

advantage of, exploited, smothered or controlled by others. It is the character that will say a clear "no" to people or invitations that do not serve your best interests. Boundaried's protection takes the form of setting and communicating clear limits. This character will signal you when someone is a taker, and help you set limits so you're not exploited by them.

This character often generates anger as a warning signal that your boundaries are not being respected. This anger will sometimes be expressed outwardly to reinforce the boundary and restore safety, but more often it prompts you to withdraw from the person or situation. This can take the form of physically leaving, or emotionally shutting down.

Boundaried preserves your ability to prioritize using your time to meet your own needs, by preventing you from taking ownership of other people's problems.

The Boundaried Insider

If Boundaried is an Insider on your Inner Team, you are all about clarity. You set, establish and maintain boundaries, and you respect the boundaries set by others. You know where you stand. You know what you think. You know what's important to you, and what's not.

You attend to your own needs. You know what fuels you and drains you, what you'll tolerate and what you won't. You don't see much point in hiding this from other people.

You are more likely than most to express an opinion that deviates from a group's consensus view. You're aware of the pressure to agree, but are not usually subject to it. You consult your own ethics, determine if it aligns with your true north. If you agree, it will be by your own choice, not from a pressure to fit in.

You take people at their word. You don't waste energy trying to read between the lines. You say what you mean, and you expect others to do the same. When others are being slippery or evasive about accountability, you will call them on it. If you determine that they cannot be trusted, you will work around them in future.

You know that you're not everyone's cup of tea. You don't need everyone to be your friend. Given the choice, you'd rather be respected than liked.

When you say yes to a request, you mean it. Saying no is relatively easy for you. You won't commit to a deadline you can't reach, or to an agreement you can't keep. That would lack integrity, and you wouldn't respect yourself if you agreed to something you had no intention of doing.

You want and need space to make up your own mind. If you feel pressured, your answer will default to "no".

You value healthy relationships, where there is space for each person to be who they are. In your heart of hearts, you are ambivalent about getting close. You prefer your relationships to include lots of room for privacy. You like time with people in small doses, with spaces in between. It costs energy to connect, and you choose to conserve what you have. You regularly experience "relational claustrophobia", the feeling that people are too close, invading your privacy, getting up in your business, being overly familiar.

You will not allow yourself to get involved in other people's dramas. You respect people enough to trust that they will find their own solutions. If they need your help, they can ask.

Your willingness to trust others is conditional. It builds slowly, from demonstrations of a willingness to honor your boundaries. You react strongly if someone breaks confidentiality.

Origins of Boundaried

Your Boundaried character came to prominence on your Inner Team to create the distance, privacy and clarity you need to thrive. Many people with a Boundaried Insider describe early environments where they were allowed little autonomy or privacy.

You decided early on that it was better to keep your thoughts to yourself, often after witnessing other people share information that was then used against them. Better to be secretive and safe than open and exploited.

You learned early on that if you said yes to helping others, there was a risk that they would not stop asking and taking. So you became cautious about what you would give. It's not that you're ungenerous as much as deliberate and measured in how you choose to help others.

When Boundaried is operating on your Inner Team without the balancing influence of Pleaser, you may find it difficult to:

- Give your time and attention generously and spontaneously.

- Express the warmth and caring you feel for others.

- Be flexible and accommodating to others' needs and preferences

- Participate in group situations where roles and group process are unclear or shift suddenly.

PROTECTOR AND TRUSTING

Integrating Protector and Trusting allows you to balance:

- Caution **and** risk-taking
- Privacy **and** openness/transparency
- Conditional trust **and** unconditional trust

THE PROTECTOR

The part of you that scans for risk, and shows you the path to safety and security.

How The Protector Protects You

The Protector is a universal character, a member of every Inner Team. Its single, crucial job is to guard your safety and security, physically, socially, financially, even spiritually. It does this by constantly scanning for threats and risks, and prompting you to respond appropriately.

The Protector responds both to threats in the present and the past. It is the part of you which remembers experiences of being terrified or threatened, and does everything it can to ensure you never experience these again.

Protector is the source of gut feelings of whether a person can be trusted. It's the Protector that tells you whether it's safe to accept an invitation to a dinner or a job interview. It's the Protector who signals you when someone is manipulating or deceiving you. It's your Protector that nudges you to read the negative reviews before you purchase a product, protecting you from a financial error. Protector operates by the principle that everything and everyone is a potential threat, until proven otherwise.

The Protector defines and polices your comfort zone, defining what's inside as safe, what's outside as unsafe. The comfortable, familiar feeling of being in your comfort zone is what a happy Protector feels like. The uncomfortable, uncertain, off-center feeling when you leave your comfort zone reflects the stirring of a Protector who wants you to be super careful in this new, unfamiliar territory.

Protector as an Insider

When the Protector operates as an Insider, your capacity to stay safe - and keep others safe - becomes an identity. Security is a primary concern and focus of attention. It constantly asks the question "What might go wrong?"

The Protector Insider is vigilance personified. It is slow to trust, believing that the world is fundamentally dangerous. To trust is to open yourself to the potential of being harmed. This produces its characteristic emotional states of worry, anxiety and fear. While the inner state of the Protector is far from peaceful, there is no character better equipped to prevent and preempt problems.

Protector Insiders want you to be prepared for anything. It will prompt you to think through worst-case scenarios, and to create plans accordingly.

The Protector worries about money, but it can bring the same level of concern to any other factor that affects safety and security, such as your health or the status of your most important relationships. Protectors approve of security systems of all kinds, from burglar alarms to unbreakable passwords. Insurance is highly valued.

When life feels like an endless battle to ward off a disaster that's just around the corner, your Protector is in charge of your

Inner Team. In the absence of the Inner Leader, the Protector is the Inner Team's default boss. It focuses your attention on what you need to do to survive, from holding down a job to having enough money for life-preserving essentials like food and shelter. Protector fears being unprepared, and can over-prepare as a result. It's not uncommon to find a Protector Insider stockpiling whatever makes you feel safer. This can be supplies like fuel and food, but it can equally well be social connections you can count on to have your back.

One of the Protector's key roles is to ensure you act appropriately. It will identify the norms of any social situation, including its unspoken rules, to determine what you need to do to be safe in that setting. Your Protector is hard at work in any situation where you notice yourself playing it safe, for example by avoiding controversial topics like politics or religion.

The Protector's Partners
Protector is unique in the way it partners with other characters on the Inner Team. Protector is the part that identifies a threat, but it is usually not the Protector who responds to it. It calls on other characters on the Inner Team to bring a solution that has worked for you in the past.

For example, the Protector will activate in response to a threat such as your boss feeling upset with you, prompting you to do something to make sure you don't get fired. It might call on your Pleaser, to appease your boss by being accommodating. It might call on your Pusher, to work even harder to prove your worth. It might call on Free Agent, to brush up your resume so you can rapidly escape to a new job. In each case, the Protector recognizes a threat, and calls upon your most proven, reliable strategies to respond to it (namely, your Insiders).

For this reason, Protector is often a behind-the-scenes character on the Inner Team. You may be less aware of the Protector than other powerful characters: you're far more likely to notice that your response to stress is to people please or withdraw, than to notice the part of you which conducted the threat evaluation which immediately preceded it.

Origins of the Protector

Protector forms early in life, to help the child discover and repeat behaviors that earn the love, approval and protection of his or her parents, and avoid their judgment, anger or sadness. These decisions about what behaviors win love and approval, and avoid pain and rejection, form into rules. The Protector's lifelong job is to remind you to follow these rules. Because its rules are tied to survival, they are very hard to change.

Those with particularly strong and active Protectors often report an early environment that was fundamentally unsafe. Those who were supposed to provide protection failed to do so, were inconsistent, or were absent altogether. The Protector steps forward to internalize the role of the protective parent.

The more threatening the early environment, the stronger the Protector tends to be in adulthood. When there's a history of trauma, the Protector can produce hyper-vigilance.

If you are part of a group that experiences prejudice (based on race, gender, gender identity, national origin, sexual orientation, religious affiliation, and more) your Protector will have been essential to your social or physical survival. It's the Protector that prompts adaptations like keeping your personal life hidden and code-switching.

When Protector is operating on your Inner Team without the balancing influence of Trusting, you may experience:

- A tendency to be guarded and suspicious, even somewhat paranoid, assuming that others cannot be trusted and are operating with negative intent towards you.

- Difficulty trusting other people enough to let your guard down, which can create challenges with experiencing closeness and intimacy in relationships.

- Distorted risk assessment: what might go wrong is magnified, what might go right is minimized or ignored altogether.

- Cautiousness and conservatism. What is known is safe, everything else is dangerous. The world narrows to what is already familiar, producing a very small comfort zone, and a marked fragility when forced outside of it.

- Defining success as the absence of threats and problems.

- Self-protective body language, such as such as raised shoulders or crossed arms.

TRUSTING

Trusting is the part of each of us which extends trust to others.

How Trusting Protects You

Trusting keeps fear at bay by looking for evidence that the world is a safe and supportive place. This character assumes that other people are basically good. Trust is given rather than earned; people are assumed to be worthy of trust until proven otherwise.

This produces an open, unguarded way of relating that allows you to build close relationships you can rely on.

Trusting supports authentic optimism, the feeling that something will go right, a deep conviction that good things are coming your way. Trusting operates from the core belief that the universe is always acting for you rather than against you. It can direct your attention to the ways you've been supported. It can reframe any problem into an opportunity. It has a "silver lining radar" that can find the thread of learning and growth that comes out of even the most challenging experiences.

Trusting is not a hyper-positive, sunshine-and-rainbows character, however. It does not try and pretend that difficult experiences aren't really that bad (that would be the Minimizer), but finds a core of trust from which to respond to whatever is happening. Think of a person finding a kind of peace in response to a difficult diagnosis, rather than shaking her fist at the heavens.

Trusting as an Insider

When Trusting is an Insider on your Inner Team, your innate optimism becomes an identity. You see yourself as a positive person, full of hope for the future. You will bring positivity, hope and optimism to groups you belong to.

Trusting Insiders are quick to lower their guard, and tend to be reluctant to keep much hidden about themselves, their agendas, their needs. Being open is your strategy to connect, and establish mutually supportive partnerships.

Because you are quick to trust other people, you tend to believe that they will do likewise, and can be surprised when others are more guarded with you. When people do let you down, you will not respond by withdrawing into a protective shell and hiding from the world. Instead, your instinct will be to reach out and see what can be done to rebuild trust.

Trusting influences your sense of what is possible in troubled or conflictual relationships. You firmly believe that trust is resilient, and can recover if breached. Forgiveness comes more easily to you than to many people. You automatically give people grace, having learned that when you believe in people, they'll often pleasantly surprise you, and rise to your expectations. A Trusting Insider assumes that others act with positive intent, even when they have a negative impact.

Where Protector is hyper-vigilant for what can go wrong, Trusting asks the opposite question: "What could go right?" In place of Protector's paranoia (the feeling that the world is conspiring against you), Trusting experiences *Pronoia*, the feeling that the world around you is conspiring to support you. Trusting can easily produce evidence of this support, such as times you needed help, and it arrived at just the right moment. This assumption of support allows you to reframe anxiety-provoking experiences like public speaking. Where Protector is armored up against the expectation of failure, Trusting is more likely to assume your audience is rooting for you to succeed than waiting for you to bomb.

Trusting is the opposite of security conscious. It's the part of you that can relax if you left your door unlocked. While this character can appear naïve, it would be more accurate to say that it reflects an unwillingness to live life on the defensive. The energy cost of guarding yourself from every possible risk is seen as too high. Rather than focusing on preventing something bad from occurring, Trusting focuses instead on your capacity to adapt if it does.

Origins of Trusting

A Trusting Insider can emerge in people whose early environment was safe, and their attachments secure. The belief that others could be trusted was internalized, and became a foundational assumption.

By contrast, it can also emerge as a reaction to circumstances in which fear was the dominant emotion. This may have taken the form of a fearful, suspicious or pessimistic parent, or a family environment characterized by distrust. Trusting emerged as a rejection of this defensive view of the world, focusing on the (rare) moments when the parent was present, support was available, and things worked out better than expected.

Whatever the origin story of your Trusting character, it will serve you as a bulwark against feeling the pain of unreliable relationships, and uncertain outcomes.

When Trusting is operating within your Inner Team without the balancing influence of Protector, you may experience:

- A tendency to overshare, assuming a level of intimacy that has not yet been developed.

- Excessive optimism, expecting best-case outcomes and being surprised when problems and challenges inevitably occur.

- Believing in other people's capacity for change, even when there is little evidence of their willingness to do so.

- Risk blindness, leading to getting caught up in get-rich-quick schemes, and the like.

- Toxic positivity

PUSHER AND BEING

Integrating Pusher and Being allows you to balance:
- Action **and** reflection
- Activity **and** rest
- Reacting quickly **and** responding wisely
- Urgency **and** patience
- Getting to a destination **and** enjoying the journey

THE PUSHER

The Pusher is the part in each of us which prompts action and generates urgency to get stuff done.

How it Protects You

The Pusher gets you into action. To the Pusher, life is a list of tasks to be completed. It keeps score by how much you get done, and how fast. The Pusher is a source of enormous power to achieve, and is a highly effective antidote to the fear of being powerless, at the effect of circumstances and forces beyond your control.

The Pusher is the solution to feeling stuck. It urges you to act, to do something to take charge. It offers the perspective that your value in the world comes from what you do, so you'd better get busy and do something to contribute. Since most workplaces reflect the Pusher's bias towards action, this character is essential to career success.

While Pusher tends to focus on career-related work, it will push on anything, from athletic work (one more set, one more lap), artistic work (one more sketch or round of edits) or even spiritual work (meditate longer, read one more personal growth book).

It has the capacity to narrow your focus to the next task on your to-do list, a successful strategy for keeping your attention distracted from other concerns. If you're always focused on work, you never have to deal with feelings like emptiness, loss or confusion.

Pusher as an Insider

The Pusher is a high-energy character with a strong sense of urgency and a desire to take action. It's the character behind the decision to get up an hour early to work out, to do that extra load of laundry before you go to bed, to push through fatigue to hit a deadline at work. Without the gifts of a strong Pusher, you wouldn't get much done. When there is lots to do, whether at home or work, the Pusher is a powerful ally and source of energy to get you into action.

The Pusher dislikes incomplete tasks, and experiences checking a task off your to-do list as a release of pressure. Pusher believes that there is always more that you could and therefore should do, meaning there will never be an end to the tasks. No matter how many you check off your list, it still feels like you haven't accomplished enough, that you should have done more. This is the paradox of the Pusher: it's the reason why you can accomplish a lot, and also the source of the feeling that you're behind and not doing enough.

The Pusher values speed, and is impatient with anything you perceive as slowing you down, from slow traffic to analysis paralysis. To the urgency-driven Pusher, faster is always better, and doing something is always better than doing nothing.

The Pusher doesn't particularly care *what* action you take, only that you are in motion, doing *something*. Pushers can push you towards being more productive at work, push your kids to get involved in and excel at every sport or activity, or push you to use every available minute of a vacation (Tennis at 9, Yoga at 10, Golf at 11).

The Pusher dislikes inaction, and gets itchy when sitting still. The Pusher places little value on activities such as mindfulness and meditation, although some Pushers have been known to push meditating more, longer and better.

The business world is dominated by unrestrained Pushers in leadership roles, demanding more and more work on shorter and shorter timelines. Because of this pattern, it's almost impossible to thrive in a business setting without a strong Pusher of your own. The Pusher creates a workplace that values task-focused action, a sense of urgency, and is driven by a fear of falling behind. Areas where many businesses struggle, such as making sufficient time for reflection, rest and renewal, reflect the Pusher's limitations.

Origins of the Pusher

Some people with strong Pushers describe an early environment in which the capacity to work hard was considered the highest of all human virtues. Work was to be pursued with an almost religious fervor, while laziness was the worst possible sin.

The Pusher emerges as a response to an environment in which love is conditional. If love is to be earned by pulling your weight around the house or achieving good grades at school, the Pusher will get you moving to achieve these results. Pusher is the ultimate Inner Team resource to support high achievement in school, both academically and in sports.

Whatever your Pusher's unique origins, it serves as a powerful form of protection against feeling stuck, trapped and powerless.

If your Pusher is operating in your Inner Team without the balancing influence of Being, you may experience:

- Difficulty switching off. A busy mind, especially in the early hours of the morning.

- Burnout, from driving yourself past the point of exhaustion

- Dissatisfaction with yourself: if more is always better, what you have already accomplished is never enough.

- Turning work into a virtue rather than a means to an end. Pusher tends to over-value the capacity to work hard and fast over all other considerations, even when that hard work has minimal impact on outcomes.

- A habit of turning rest into work, by over-scheduling your weekend or vacation time.

- Tension headaches

BEING
Being is the part of each of us which has the capacity to live in the present moment, to rest, reflect, renew and relax.

How Being Protects You
Being protects you from working yourself into a state of exhaustion. It's the character who reminds you that rest and renewal are necessities, not luxuries to indulge in when all the work is done.

Where Pusher produces overwork and driving yourself past your limits, Being offers access to the wisdom of pausing. It offers a counterpoint to the conventional, Pusher-influenced belief that nothing is achieved without effort, drive and willpower. Being's approach is about emergence, allowing, creating the conditions for what is desired to come forth naturally, at its right time.

Being calms anxiety and fear, bringing attention away from what might happen in future to what is occurring right now. Because there is nowhere you need to be, it is a balm to worries that you should be somewhere other than where you are. When the fear emerges, for example, that you should be further ahead in your career by now, Being returns energy to what is possible right now in the job you have.

Being as an Insider

Being brings the gifts of composure, patience and non-reactivity. It supports the capacity to pause, re-center, to re-establish an internal coherence between heart, mind and spirit from which wise action can emerge. It aims to reduce internal pressure, in the knowledge that a relaxed mind is more creative and productive.

If Pusher is the accelerator, Being is the brake. If Pusher is "human doing", then Being is "human being". Being is not averse to action and achievement, but its destination is fundamentally different. Being's deepest aspiration is to be fully present in the moment, right here and right now. Pusher is focused on getting somewhere, as fast as possible. Being knows that there is nowhere you have to go. Joy isn't achieved by arriving at some future destination, but by savoring what is occurring right now, wherever you are. Being conveys the capacity to enjoy the journey, to stop and smell the proverbial roses.

Being is naturally reflective. When Being is in charge of a decision, for example, it will get quiet, make space for you to tune into your internal signals for which option will best serve your intentions. Being offers the wisdom that no action can be the wisest course, that patience is rewarded. Where Pusher always wants to do something right now, Being can sit back, observe, reflect and allow clarity to emerge in time. The Pusher's rule is "Don't just stand there, do something!", but Being's rule is "Don't just do something, stand there!"

Being is naturally inclined towards meditative practice in all its forms, including meditation, mindfulness, journaling, and forms of conscious movement like Yoga. Professionally, Being will be drawn towards roles that require a quality of presence and conscious intention – such as facilitation, counseling, coaching or ministry. Being's superpower in relationships is the ability to listen patiently, without the need to fix.

Being is often prominent in artists, writers, creatives, and other similar roles where inspiration and flow are crucial.

Being's Origins

People with a strong Being character often describe an early environment that was over-stimulating in some way, like a chaotic household. Being emerged as a way to create an inner calm amid the storm.

Being can also originate from an experience of the hollowness of worldly achievement. When you're surrounded by people who are outwardly successful but inwardly empty, Being offers a contrasting path focused on inner rather than outer richness.

Whatever the origin story of your Being character, it provides presence, depth and the capacity to find stillness no matter what is occurring around you.

When Being operates on your Inner Team without the balancing influence of Pusher, you may experience:

- Inertia, finding it difficult to get yourself started. This can produce procrastination or avoidance.

- You can be patient to a fault, creating an impression of passivity or complacency.

- You can disappear into your inner world, feeling reluctant to translate vision or desire into action.

- Navel contemplation, over-thinking without intention to act, waiting for inspiration to strike

- Feeling rather aimless about goals/outcomes. Enjoys the journey, to the detriment of the destination.

RATIONAL AND FEELING

Integrating Rational and Feeling will allow you to balance:

- Reason **and** Passion
- A clear mind **and** an open heart
- Objectivity **and** Subjectivity
- Quantitative analysis **and** qualitative assessment

RATIONAL

Rational is the part of each of us which uses intellect, analysis and rational deduction to make sense of the world.

How Rational Protects You

Rational deploys the power of the intellect to make a confusing world more understandable. It constantly asks, "Why?" and searches for reliable, truthful answers. By sharpening and refining your mind, you are protected from being fooled, outsmarted or manipulated with false or misleading information.

Rational constantly gathers and evaluates information, believing that the more you know, the safer you will be. It organizes information into categories, forming theories and hypotheses to explain what you're experiencing. When rational is in charge, your mind is helping you create order out of chaos.

The Rational Insider

The Rational Insider produces an analytical way of engaging with the world. Who you are is defined by what you think, and your worth established by how much you know. Being good is synonymous with being smart.

You take pride in the extraordinary instrument that is your mind, thinking and pondering, probing and proving. Sometimes you get so preoccupied by your thoughts that the world around you disappears for a while.

For the Rational Insider, reading and studying are as natural as breathing. This character prefers non-fiction over fiction, quantitative over qualitative data. It likes to measure, to quantify the world, to discover underlying formulas and algorithms, the equations that govern how things work. Numbers make sense: they're satisfyingly precise.

The Rational Insider has a superpower of observing and analyzing, in order to gather and make sense of data. It will constantly ask questions, probe and test, challenging the world to reveal its secrets. You discover the world fact by fact, idea by idea, until a map begins to form in your mind of how it all works. Each new piece of knowledge adds detail to the map, until the world makes more sense to you. You delight in figuring out patterns, and finding ways to test your conclusions.

The Rational Insider is puzzled that other people seem to be able to navigate the world without thinking as hard as you do. How do they know, for sure, what decision to make? Have they really considered all the variables, contemplated all the scenarios? You don't like to accept what you're told, preferring to think for yourself, drawing your own conclusions.

When you see other people experiencing confusion, your impulse is to offer them what you most want in such moments: to understand why. As a result, you lead with your mind in your relationships, expressing caring by sharing information and offering explanations. You may feel compelled to correct what you believe is faulty thinking or an erroneous conclusion.

You are likely to be someone that others turn to as a source of reliable information and critical insight. Over time, you have embraced this role as the source of your value. You thoroughly enjoy being around your fellow thinkers, those who share your preference for questioning and challenging, because they make you even smarter.

Your quantitative, analytical mind equips you to understand the physical world, but it doesn't work quite as well in the domain of human relationships. When you are asked about your feelings, you may find them hard to discern. You know you have them, but you're not convinced they're as important as others seem to think. You think about your feelings sometimes, even talk about them, but you don't always see the point of expressing them. Feelings are too nebulous to measure and analyze, so you direct your attention to what you can define and grasp with your intellect.

Origins of Rational

Rational often comes to prominence on the Inner Team as a way to manage emotional sensitivity. You may have been told early on that you were "too sensitive", and internalized the message that showing your emotions is unsafe. Rational appears to be cool, objective and detached, but the internal reality is often quite the opposite.

The more you occupy your attention with thinking, the less you have to stay present with painful emotions you feel. Your family may have modeled this for you, operating by an unspoken agreement to keep emotions strictly concealed.

Education systems often reinforce this pattern, rewarding students for their intellectual capacities, and overlooking emotional and social intelligence.

When Rational is operating on your Inner Team without the balancing influence of Feeling, you may experience:

- A tendency to overthink, talking yourself into and out of decisions, sometimes to the point of analysis paralysis.
- A difficulty discerning the emotional drivers of your decisions and opinions.
- Difficulty with distinguishing one emotion from another
- Thinking about feelings rather than feeling them
- A tendency to dismiss or overlook what can't be measured quantitatively, valuing empirical data to the exclusion of intuitive data.
- Responding to pain in others with explanations, information and analysis, when the moment calls for empathy or compassion.
- Defensiveness about your ideas, the reflex to prove you're right, sometimes at the cost of relationship or learning.
- Living in your head, leading to a feeling of isolation

FEELING
Feeling is the sensitive and receptive part of each of us, whose first language is emotion.

How Feeling Protects You
Feeling is the part that organizes your reactions and decisions according to the dictates of the heart. It's this part which allows you to name what you are feeling. Without access to this character, you would be unable to sense and respond to the stirring of joy, or the first shiver of fear.

Feeling is deeply sensitive and empathic. Its energetic field is extended, to reach out to others to feel what they are feeling. Combined with the capacity to tune in to your inner state, this produces a finely honed intuition. You may not know *how* you know, but you know. This will show up in uncannily accurate first impressions, hunches and unexplained impulses.

Feeling is a source of passion, and can bring aliveness and vitality to the most mundane experiences. It can lift you out of a state of boredom or disinterest by opening your heart to be moved by what you experience.

Feeling helps you be fully seen. It enables openness and authenticity, allowing you to engage with others as you truly are.

The Feeling Insider

If Feeling is an Insider on your Inner Team, your heart over-flows with feelings. A butterfly's wings can thrill you, a sad movie can devastate you, a friend's successes can fill you with shared joy. You are moved by what you see, your eyes only ever a blink away from tears of joy or sadness.

A Feeling Insider brings an exquisite sensitivity. At a glance, you can tell what someone else is feeling, and would often feel a stirring of that same emotion in your own heart. You know instinctively when someone is not telling you the truth; it sounds in you like a false note in a chord. That sensitivity gives you the superpower of saying or doing just the right thing at the right time to salve a wounded heart or calm an anxious soul.

At times, the Feeling Insider can become flooded. There are so many feelings, it can get too much. The emotions are demanding to be felt, and create pressure to express them through move-ment, activity, or a good, cathartic cry. As an Insider, Feeling will often be confused that some people seem to be able to ignore or deny their feelings. It is simply not an option for you.

Whether you are feeling unease when meeting a new person or a sensation of warmth in your chest when visiting your favorite coffee shop, your feelings are reliable guides. On the rare occasion you disregard their whispers of information and allow your mind to make your choices, regret will inevitably follow. Your mind creates a very different picture of the world than your heart, which is consistently oriented towards where fulfillment and connection are available. You are more likely to act on the promptings of faith than according to a pre-made plan.

The Feeling Insider can feel different, marginalized and misunderstood, as if you're playing by an entirely different set of rules than other people. When they claim to be objective or evidence-based, you see them as blind to the ways their heart is leading their mind. You are piercingly aware of the damage it causes when people separate their head and heart, leaving them unaware of their motives and detached from human caring. In this divided state, people are capable of doing great harm, justifying their heartlessness with excuses such as, "It's just business."

You are not unaware of the value of critical thinking, but place more trust in your intuition to make connections that are beyond the reach of your mind. When facing a big decision, pros and cons lists provide little clarity, often confusing you further. Your decision making is more internal: imagine each option, and let your heart tell you whether it is right. A rising, expansive energy and a sense of peace means the decision will serve you well. A contracted, uneasy feeling indicates it will not, no matter what the mind may say.

Origins of Feeling

You learned early on to read the emotional state of the adults in your life, for example noticing the first rumblings of anger which might be about to explode. By noticing these, you learned to guard your tender heart, knowing when to run away, and when it was safe to stick around.

Your early environment may have been populated with adults who struggled to express their emotions. You absorbed what they were feeling, and it would sometimes be expressed through you.

When Feeling is operating without the balancing influence of Rational, you may experience:

• Dwelling on feelings until they magnify and feel overwhelming.

• Moodiness

• Taking others' comments personally

• When upset, it can be hard for you to separate facts (what's objectively true) from stories (what you make those facts mean).

• Being an "emotional sponge", taking others' feelings into your own heart and body, to the point where it can become difficult to distinguish what's mine from what's yours.

• A tendency to believe what makes you feel good, without reality-checking it with contradictory data.

• A reluctance to set measurable objectives and goals, preferring to be guided by your felt sense that you are making progress.

• First impressions and hunches are so strong that you may find yourself gathering evidence that they are true (confirmation bias).

RESPONSIBLE AND PLAYFUL

Integrating Responsible and Playful allows you to balance:

- Seriousness **and** play
- Being consistent **and** being spontaneous
- Honoring commitments **and** keeping your options open
- Adulting **and** Kidding

RESPONSIBLE

Responsible is the part of each of us which is committed to fulfilling obligations and keeping your word.

How Responsible Protects You

Responsible brings stability to your life and your relationships. By supporting your ability to consistently show up and fulfill your commitments, it helps you earn and sustain trust and inclusion, in family, community and the workplace. Without Responsible, society would not function. It depends completely on individuals who keep their commitments, take ownership and follow through.

For Responsible, love is a verb. It's something you do, not just something you feel. To Responsible, love is showing up for someone else, tools in hand, with a willing heart.

The Responsible Insider

When Responsible is an Insider on your Inner Team, you will automatically take ownership. This could look like pulling your weight when work needs to be done, paying your fair share of a financial commitment, or being the kind of person who says,

"The buck stops with me." A Responsible Insider will demon-strate the gifts of practicality, pragmatism and groundedness, and a willingness to hold oneself accountable.

To the Responsible character, inclusion in any group is earned by showing up, taking ownership, and walking your talk. Responsible does not make commitments lightly. Once a com-mitment is made, you feel obliged to follow through. Responsible believes that a choice cannot be unmade.

Responsible brings your attention to all the ways in which others depend on you, and organizes priorities in order to live up to those commitments. It is fueled by a strong sense of obligation.

This can express as protectiveness of others under your care, taking responsibility for their wellbeing. It can also produce dil-igence in following the traditions of a religious or spiritual prac-tice. Whatever area of life it touches, Responsible sees fulfilling your obligations as the way to be worthy.

As well as helping you keep your commitments, Responsible can also orient you towards taking ownership of your impact on others in your relationships. When you unintentionally hurt someone else, it's Responsible which takes this seriously, and ensures you learn from the experience.

Responsible is the character behind a decision to "turn pro" and make the shift from a hobby to a vocation. It's the difference between being someone who writes and an author, a person who paints and an artist. It doesn't, of course, confer skill in any of these activities, but it provides the energy and intention to take the practice seriously. Wherever you are dedicated, consistent and serious, you're being guided by your Responsible character.

Responsible is one of the characters in the Inner Team which receives almost unconditional social approval. In a world where being responsible is synonymous with being good, to be irresponsible is to be bad. Responsible will do almost anything to prevent you from being seen as irresponsible.

Many of your successes in life can be traced back to your superpower of being consistent. You naturally follow author Victoria Erickson's maxim that *"Consistency is an underappreciated form of intentional magic disguised as a mundane doing."* (from "Edge of Wonder")

Origins of the Responsible Character

The Responsible character eventually develops in almost all adults, as we adapt to a world that expects us to earn our own living, to be individually accountable, to meaningfully contribute to society.

For some, it becomes a major player on the Inner Team long before they reach adulthood. Many people with a strong Responsible character faced a family situation in which they had to take on adult-like responsibilities very early in life. For example, being responsible for caring for a younger sibling or sick relative, or being asked to contribute financially to the family from an early age.

Responsible can also become an Insider for people who faced unreliable, inconsistent parenting. Responsible is an effective response to ensuring an early experience of food insecurity never gets repeated in adult life.

Whatever your unique story, Responsible develops to guard against the pain of having abandoned or neglected someone else.

When Responsible is operating in your Inner Team without the balancing influence of Playful, you may experience:

- A feeling of heaviness, joylessness, all work and no play. A belief that life is an unrelenting burden, less a joyful journey and more a determined slog forward to meet one's obligations.

- The feeling that you have no choice. Your actions are pre-determined by the obligation to fulfill commitments made in the past. You live in a world of *shoulds, have-to's* and *musts*.

- Seeing pleasure, play and rest as self-indulgent luxuries.

PLAYFUL
Playful is the eternal child within each of us, the part which can have fun anywhere, and turn anything into a game.

How Playful Protects You
Playful protects you from taking yourself too seriously. Even in the darkest moments, Playful can help us release tension by having a good laugh at the absurdity of the world and the silliness of the people in it (yourself included). For Playful, there is nothing as cathartic as a good laugh, and no better way to restore your sense of perspective.

When you are feeling restricted and limited, Playful helps you restore a sense of freedom. Playful will turn the most mundane, repetitive task into a game.

Playful connects you with others. For Playful, the way to create relationship is by being fun to be around. Playful doesn't wait for joy to arrive; it brings joy into every moment.

When Playful is an Insider

If Responsible sees life as a burden to carry, Playful sees it as a magnificent, unpredictable and delightful adventure. Where Responsible is focused on following through on commitments from the past, Playful is all about what's possible right now, in the present moment.

When Playful is an Insider on your inner team, you have access to innocence, a willingness to shrug off assumptions from the past and operate from a beginner's mind.

Playful represents the eternal child in you, with all its mercurial capacity for change. If you've ever entertained the thought "I just can't adult today!", that's the Playful character asking for the freedom to live more in the moment.

A Playful Insider has the gift of child-like curiosity. Think of a five-year-old exploring the fascinating creatures in tide pools at the beach, or up to her elbows in finger paints. In adult roles, Playful can show up as the inventor tinkering in her garage, or as an artist in her studio, following wherever her imagination takes her. Playful will love any role requiring innovation, imagination, humor and experimentation.

In the presence of people who take themselves too seriously, Playful will poke fun, crack jokes, anything to restore a sense of perspective. Playful can be mischievous, liking to puncture pomposity, self-importance or an inflated ego.

Playful's relationships tend to be based less on meeting each other's needs, and more on enjoying each other. Conversation will tend towards improvisational comedy rather than deep discussion.

Playful's rules for living tend to be simple: the world has an endless array of delights available for you to discover. Don't delay pleasure (eat dessert first!). Never take advice from unhappy people.

Playful's spirit is captured perfectly in James Boswell's famous retort to Samuel Johnson: *"I have tried in my time to be a philosopher, but I don't know how, cheerfulness was always breaking in."*

Playful's Origins

Playful is a universal character, because it represents the spirit of a childhood stage which is magical, imaginative and endlessly creative. Adults who remain in close contact with their Playful character often describe a moment where they looked at the way most grown-ups live, and decided it was simply too boring to be tolerated. Playful becomes a strategy to escape a life burdened by duty, obligation and unending responsibility.

For some people whose early experience was particularly demanding and difficult, imagination can represent the only escape route.

When Playful operates on your Inner Team in the absence of the balancing influence of Responsible, you may experience:

- Reluctance to make commitments, or any promises that might constrain your freedom in future.

- Inconsistency and unpredictability, which can create a perception that you are unreliable

- Constant searching for the next high, but an inability to feel satisfied by what you find.

- An allergy to the parts of life that feel mundane, repetitive or routine.

RULE FOLLOWER AND REBEL

Integrating Rebel and Rule Follower allows you to balance:
- Conventional **and** Unconventional
- Deference to authority **and** trusting your own authority
- Rigid compliance **and** individual determination

RULE FOLLOWER
Rule Follower is the part of each of us that conscientiously follows rules in order to feel safe and above criticism.

How it Protects You
The Rule Follower protects you from judgment by keeping you firmly on the right side of law, convention and precedent. It operates from the belief that rules exist for good reasons, and that authorities who set rules can be trusted. You feel safest when you adhere to standards and comply with regulations.

In addition to helping you comply with external rules, the Rule Follower supports your capacity to be in a state of personal integrity, in which your behavior completely aligns with your own principles, standards and expectations. To say one thing and do another feels like an act of self-betrayal. Being someone who walks their talk, who is free of hypocrisy, is a source of pride. Achieving this state of personal integrity defend you against criticism.

The Rule Follower also operates at times as a rule maker. Whatever rule of behavior you make for yourself, you will follow it as consistently as you can. Your Rule Follower supports your capacity to repeat what works, from a workout routine to a time management strategy.

Rule Follower as an Insider

When Rule Follower is an Insider, you automatically look for rules to follow. This might take the form of seeking a process or procedure to follow at work, paying careful attention to the safety demonstration on a plane, or carefully reading the instruction manual before activating a new device. Following rules takes on urgent importance, because they feel like a bulwark against chaos, and can be imbued with life and death importance. Choosing to disobey a rule is seen not only as foolish or arrogant, but heretical.

Where Rebel can be advice-resistant, Rule Follower is particularly receptive to advice when it comes from a reputable source. Your search for rules to follow will often lead you to seek experts whose advice you can trust.

When you are in a situation where you must break one rule to comply with another, you may experience significant distress. For example, imagine you were sitting at an intersection, waiting for the red light to turn green, but it does not do so for two cycles. The cars behind you are honking. The road is clear. Do you go through the red light? This would be a pragmatic decision for many people, but generates real distress for the Rule Follower.

This character brings the gift of impartiality, the principle that justice is blind. This character loves the idea of standards that are fair and just, and therefore should be applied universally.

Rule Followers are natural stewards of culture. Whether in a family, an organization or an institution, cultural norms that have worked for the previous generation are passed on to the next as rules to follow. It's the Rule Follower character who shoulders the responsibility to ensure that the next generation is given positive rules to follow.

The Rule Follower Insider will give what you most want to receive: clear directions, standards and expectations. This character will work diligently to ensure those rules are clearly defined and spelled out, and communicated with precision. Unsurprisingly, this character has an affinity for professions that serve as stewards and enforcers of rules, such as lawyers, law enforcement personnel, compliance and audit professionals.

Rule Follower takes a generally dim view of risk-taking. The idea of winging it, in almost any domain of life, is inconceivable.

The Rule Follower sees a world that is chaotic, unpredictable, and full of mixed messages, and sets out to restore a feeling of rightness, integrity, stability and clarity.

Rule Follower commonly partners with two other characters. The Judge, who is quick to criticize those who don't follow the rules, and Ordinary, who wants to remind you that rules apply to you and that you're not special and above the law.

Rule Follower's Origins

You may have grown up in a home where obedience and deference to authority was expected and enforced.

You may have watched someone close to you (a rebellious sibling, for example) face rejection, judgment and exile from the tribe, and made an internal decision never to let this happen to you.

Whatever circumstances brought it to prominence on your Inner Team, the Rule Follower protects the young, vulnerable little girl or boy within you who's frightened by not knowing what to do, and wants orientation and guidance to feel safe.

When Rule Follower is operating on your Inner Team without the balancing influence of Rebel, you may experience:

- A feeling that it's up to you to be the standard bearer for what is right and good.

- The mental habit of comparing reality unfavorably to the ideal picture in your mind, in which everyone follows the rules, to the benefit of all.

- Difficulty innovating, cleaving to what's tried and true over something new and unproven. If it's not broken, why fix it?

- Feeling offended when people who don't follow the rules get rewarded, and righteous anger when you notice people operating as if they were above the law. It feels deeply unjust and unfair.

- A preference for black-and-white thinking, preferring the moral certainty of good/bad, right/wrong, legal/illegal, allowing you to know for sure that you are on the right side of the rules.

- An Inner Critic that will come down hard on any impulse you feel to break a rule, be bad, go against tradition.

- While you try very hard to be good, you may find yourself oddly fascinated by "bad boys" and "bad girls". You might be repelled or attracted, but you'll find them hard to ignore.

THE REBEL

The Rebel is the part of each of us which wants to experience the freedom to make individual choices.

How it Protects You

The Rebel is hypervigilant for anything that feels like an attempt to control, coerce or limit your freedom. It will activate at the first indication that you are being controlled, and will prompt behavior that demonstrates that you are in charge of your own choices. It encourages freedom to think and act independently of rules, conventions and traditions. It's the part that will deliberately choose to go in through the out door, to zig when everyone else zags.

The Rebel protects the vulnerable part of you which carries a fear of being controlled or dominated. This fear can be intense, almost panic-inducing. The words, "You're not the boss of me!" are never far from the lips of the rebel.

By helping you stand out from the crowd, the Rebel can garner attention. It is typically untroubled if this attention is negative. The Rebel will sometimes keep score by paying attention to who you piss off: if you irritate the conformists around you, you must be doing something right.

The Rebel stands against the misuse of power, and carries an innate distrust of authority. To the Rebel, compliant, unquestioning conformity means that authorities win, and this is unacceptable.

The Rebel lives by Frank Sinatra's famous refrain, "I did it my way."

When Rebel is an Insider

The Rebel Insider is an individualist, seeking to chart his or her own course in the world, to think for himself or herself. As such, it can produce judgmental reactions to rule followers, or anyone who prefers a more conventional life. Obedience to convention is interpreted not as a reasonable choice, but as a deficiency of independent thought.

Rebel lives by the maxim that rules are made to be broken, and boats are meant to be rocked. There is an automatic skepticism about consensus beliefs and assumptions. Where the Rule Follower uses the past as a predictor of the future, the Rebel believes that rules from the past should be left in the past.

The Rebel Insider is uniquely equipped to question assumptions. Sacred cows are distinctly unsafe around the Rebel, who is constitutionally unable to accept the status quo, and feels that it must be challenged. As a result, the Rebel is less likely to be swayed by social pressure or groupthink.

The Rebel is a reactive character, needing something to push against, something to disagree with, something to resist or fight. The Rebel's identity is formed around what you are not. This habit of pushing against rules can become so automatic that people with a strong Rebel Insider will even find themselves rebelling against their own plans. The need to be free of all forms of control can be so compulsive that even self-control is resisted.

The Rebel will cut off his nose to spite his face. Even when breaking a rule will be immediately detrimental, experiencing oneself as free is more important than any negative consequence that may arise. The threat of punishment holds minimal sway over the threat of being controlled.

Rebel's disdain for authority makes it hard to fit in jobs that have a clear power hierarchy. Rebels are drawn to roles where they experience more freedom, and are more likely than most to choose to be their own boss.

Rebellion is a normal developmental stage for teenagers, but there's far more to the Rebel than an angry teenager fighting his parents' world. It's the Rebel who can free you from conventional assumptions to see a problem in a new way, to challenge accepted wisdom. To innovate, especially in an established field, requires a bit of rebel energy. The willingness to be deliberately provocative and challenging is found in a lot of ground-breaking artists, inventors and innovators.

Origins of the Rebel

The Rebel emerges as a response to difficult experiences with authority. Sometimes an early authority figure turns out to be unreliable, hypocritical, and unworthy of trust. More commonly, there are early experiences of the misuse of power and authority to suppress individuality.

When Rebel is operating on your Inner Team without the balancing influence of Rule Follower, you may experience:

- Trouble with authorities, and a pattern of defiant behavior

- Knowing what you stand <u>against</u> is far harder than knowing what you stand <u>for</u>).

- The feeling that rules don't apply to you.

- Taking a contrary position to gain attention and feel powerful, rather than because it's a deeply held belief. This can confuse others about what you truly stand for.

- Difficulty with collaborative, team-based work.

SPECIAL AND ORDINARY

Integrating Ordinary and Special will allow you to balance:
- The desire to belong **and** the desire to stand out
- What's unique to you **and** shared, common experience
- Leading from the front **and** leading from behind

SPECIAL

Special is the part of each of us which wants to stand out and be seen as unique and precious.

How Special Protects You

Special protects you from feeling invisible, overlooked and ignored. It activates in response to the fear that you are forgettable, promoting your uniqueness, so you can be seen, heard, valued and appreciated.

Special empowers you not only to be visible, but to shine so brightly that your uniqueness cannot be ignored. It ensures that you will express yourself in a way that allows you to stand out from any crowd.

The Special Insider

The Special Insider thrives on attention, which it earns by being original, creative and self-expressed. This character insists that you are <u>not</u> like everyone else. It demands that you be different and distinctive, from the clothes you wear to the attitudes you espouse. Everything you say or do must express your unique style.

The Special Insider has an allergy to "basic". Why choose vanilla, when there are so many other more interesting flavors?

Why accept beige walls when you can choose a color that captures a mood? Why parrot conventional beliefs, when you can think for yourself? To Special, the idea of conventional wisdom is an oxymoron: if it's conventional, it can't possibly be wise. You may find yourself automatically rejecting conventional advice, believing that it doesn't apply to you, because you're different.

You expect yourself to be original, to break new ground. When you achieve the kind of originality and authentic self-expression you aspire to, it's glorious. But for much of the time, you carry a nagging anxiety that you're not creative enough, or that you're really rather boring. You will work so hard to disprove this that you will often exhaust yourself.

While you love being the center of attention, you also want others to experience this high. This character has the superpower of being a genius spotter, capable of seeing someone's unique gifts and talents, even when they cannot see it themselves. You can apply this same skill to the design of a room or the marketing of a product, intuitively knowing which distinctive features to emphasize.

The Special Insider will keep you from feeling invisible, but it may leave you feeling profoundly lonely. The feeling that you're different can make you wonder whether anyone truly understands you. You may feel that you don't fit in anywhere. No matter how much you have in common with a group, you often feel like an outsider.

The belief that you need to be special and different to be worthy is a fertile feeding ground for the Inner Critic. It leads to feelings of shame about your ordinariness, from what you eat to what you wear to how you spend your time.

Origins of Special

Special tends to come to prominence on the Inner Team in people who grew up in an environment where everyone was treated the same. Adults who were not attuned to your individual needs left you feeling misunderstood. Attention may have been in short supply. Special emerged as a solution to help you stand out, have your needs recognized, to feel seen and understood, and most of all, valued.

At the other extreme, Special can also emerge for people who grew up in families where the parents were super ambitious for their children, and lean towards being over-attentive. You internalized the message that you must be a unique talent or a precocious genius to be worthy. Being a good student or a supportive friend wasn't enough to earn you any attention.

Specialness pervades cultures that value individualism. The messages to dream big, never settle and stand out are everywhere, reinforced by cultural narratives, marketing and media imagery. Ordinary's capacity to live in gratitude for what you already have and experience the joy of the everyday is almost heretical, because it's difficult to sell you something if you don't buy into the narrative of specialness.

When Special is operating on your Inner Team without the balancing influence of Ordinary, you may experience:

- A feeling that you're somehow diminished if other people share the same gifts as you.

- An Inner Critic who demands uniqueness and originality, and shames anything that doesn't reach that standard, from art to clothing to opinions.

- A reflex to reject conventional advice and standard solutions
- A feeling of being alone and misunderstood, even when receiving positive attention.
- An intense fear of being seen as mediocre, boring, unremarkable or ordinary.
- An unwillingness to accept that you fit in any box or category, a rejection of labels.
- A subtle kind of egotism, in which feeling different crosses an invisible threshold into feeling superior.

ORDINARY
Ordinary is the part of each of us which finds joy in the everyday, and delights in your similarities to other people.

How Ordinary Protects You
Ordinary protects you from the dangers of standing out and drawing attention to yourself. No character is better adapted to help you fade into the background, to safely blend in and avoid negative attention.

Ordinary is a salve to feeling isolated or separate. By focusing on the ways in which you and other people are similar rather than different, it supports the feeling that you are connected, part of one human family. Ordinary makes it possible to feel a sense of belonging.

The Ordinary Insider
Ordinary finds joy in day-to-day routines, discovers beauty in the mundane and draws real sustenance from the activities and relationships of a simple, unremarkable life.

When Ordinary is operating as an Insider on your Inner Team, you walk a path of modesty and humility. In a society that celebrates striving for more, you discover joy in the everyday experience of belonging, being part of your community, making your modest contribution to the daily turn of life. You are nourished by the kind of simple pleasures which are available every day. You thrive on the beauty of a sunrise, a perfectly ripe piece of fruit, the comforting hug of a loved one. To you, this is enough. It's all you ever wanted. Ordinary's secret to happiness is to live in gratitude for what you have.

You may feel puzzled by people who seem to endlessly strive for more, when they already have everything they need. You're largely immune to the kind of marketing that promises that a product will get you noticed, envied by others, or express your unique individuality. The idea of trying to stand out and be better than others feels wrong, because you know that you are fundamentally alike.

You instinctively recognize that beneath surface differences, most people have similar aspirations, feel similar fears, experience similar challenges. The truth that we are all one is in your bones. This enables you to connect easily with people who are outwardly different than you. Knowing yourself to be part of the human family is the bedrock of your sense of safety.

The Ordinary Insider is well adapted to thrive in team environments. You don't need much attention, and are happy to play a background role, making space for others to take center stage. For all your contributions to your team, however, you may be hesitant to accept credit, take the lead or apply for a promotion, although this may not feel like much of a loss to you.

When you are asked your opinion, you may experience some

awkwardness and self-doubt about expressing it, particularly if you're the lone voice expressing it. You may be somewhat embarrassed by attention, and feel a reluctance to self-promote.

Origins of Ordinary

Ordinary emerges as a strategy to stay safe in families where standing out, in any form, was met not with celebration but with criticism. You may have had experiences where a parent or other adult in authority tried to put you in your place. The words "Who do you think you are!" may have particular resonance. Whatever form this admonishment took, the message was clear: don't get too full of yourself, know your place, and never, ever brag.

Sometimes, Ordinary developed when you had a sibling who demanded a great deal of attention, whether through a particular talent, or special needs. Ordinary helps you adapt to the scarcity of attention, allowing you to function without it, to not be a burden on your parents.

Whatever the circumstances that prompted the development of Ordinary in your Inner Team, you will have internalized the message that it's safer to ask for little and enjoy what you have. You don't ask for any kind of special treatment. You prefer to understate your contributions and deflect attention away from yourself.

When Ordinary is operating without the balancing influence of Special, you may experience:

- A feeling that you need to hide your light, that it will be too much for others, that your shining diminishes others.

- Difficulty accepting praise, fearing that to do so is prideful, even boastful.

- You may feel the impulse to cut down "tall poppies" by reminding prideful people they're not different or special.

WARRIOR AND PEACEMAKER

Integrating Warrior and Peacemaker allows you to balance:

- Power of standing firm **and** power of yielding
- Confronting **and** allowing
- Challenge **and** acceptance
- Fighting necessary battles **and** keeping the peace

WARRIOR

The Warrior is the part of each of us which wields power through direct, principled action.

How Warrior Protects You

Warrior protects you from being controlled, coerced or dominated, defending yourself with fierceness and potency. It is a character that achieves safety by being the aggressor, facing threats directly.

The Warrior has a very physical presence. It will take up space, stand for a principle, demand to have its intense energy met. It responds to any hint of a challenge by getting bigger, leaning forward, and speaking loudly.

Warrior can use any type of power in service of self-protection. It will use the positional power of formal authority, the relational power of friendship and affiliation, even the spiritual power of acting on principle.

The Warrior Insider

Warrior Insiders confer courage. There's enormous power to act in the face of fear. The energy of Warrior is forceful, even unstoppable. The Warrior Insider typically has easy access to anger, relishing the sense of power that comes with it.

There's a willingness to confront and challenge, and conflict is experienced as both necessary and relieving. When this character is an Insider, you may seek out conflict, to look for battles that allow you an outlet for your intense protective energy. Warrior Insiders are quick to judge what they perceive as weakness, passivity or complacency.

Warrior can produce aggressiveness, but it's first and foremost about protection. You will be assertive in both guarding your own boundaries, and in protecting those who you perceive as being unable to protect themselves.

Warrior Insiders communicate in a way that's direct, straightforward and candid. This character is intolerant of withholding, of leaving things unsaid, and would rather deal with a conflict now than minimize or defer it.

Warrior Insiders can be black-and-white in their thinking. The Warrior can see the world as made up of good guys and bad guys, us and them. With maturity, Warrior seems to move from fighting *against* bad guys, reorienting to fighting *for* principles, for what matters most.

Origins of Warrior

You may have grown up in an environment where you had no one to take care of or protect you, leaving you no choice but to step up and protect yourself. You may have sensed that admitting you were scared would be dangerous, concluding it's safer to be scary than to be scared. You internalized the belief that showing up big, strong and dominant would guard you against being dominated.

Whatever the specific circumstances that led to the development of your Warrior, it offers you an enormous source of power you can use to keep yourself and others safe.

If Warrior is operating on your Inner Team without the balancing influence of Peacemaker, you may experience:

- A tendency to fight against rather than fight for.
- Judgment of people who won't share their thoughts or express an opinion, or anyone who seems complacent about issues that matter to you.
- Over-indexing on directness in your communication. Your natural candor can become blunt confrontational.
- Difficulty compromising, which feels like losing.

THE PEACEMAKER
The Peacemaker is the part of each of us which seeks and creates harmony.

How Peacemaker Protects You
Peacemaker protects by making you smaller, less visible, less of a threat. It adopts a way of relating which is undemanding, non-confrontational and easy-going. When this character is present, there's an easy positivity that can make differences and disagreements seem smaller and less important.

It is the part of you that can de-escalate a conflict. It will steer you away from the kinds of comments or reactions which would throw fuel on the proverbial fire, and will go as far as completely silencing you to accomplish this. It sees saying and doing nothing as a way to stay safe: it's the instinctive reaction to freeze, as opposed to fight or flee.

The Peacemaker Insider

The Peacemaker has a superpower of creating safety for others, by being non-judgmental, accepting, and appreciative of multiple points of view. You have the capacity to make others feel seen, heard and understood, while you remain safely invisible.

When the Peacemaker is operating as an Insider on your Inner Team, you strive to maintain harmony, reduce interpersonal tension, and keep the peace. You find conflict upsetting, and avoid it when you can, because it creates a feeling of distance and disconnection. The Peacemaker carries a core belief that conflict causes harm, that it damages relationship, and therefore it should be avoided if at all possible. In the absence of real resolution of conflict, Peacemaker will settle for a kind of false harmony that comes from avoiding problems and smoothing over differences.

Your Peacemaker has several strategies to keep the peace. First, it will bring your attention to what you have in common with others, minimizing disagreements and magnifying where you agree.

Secondly, Peacemaker will direct your attention away from yourself, and onto others. You may find yourself naturally accommodating to the preferences of others, to avoid experiencing the tension of wanting different things. This pattern is so automatic, many people with a Peacemaker Insider have a hard time knowing what they want or need, let alone asserting these in their relationships.

What Peacemaker wants you to experience is a sense of unity, the knowledge that we are all fundamentally alike. As a result, you're less likely than most to get drawn into "us and them" disagreements. You find it easy to sympathize with both sides. This ability to stay neutral, to set aside your personal opinions and agendas, makes Peacemaker a natural mediator.

The Peacemaker in partnership with the Patriarch creates a distinctive "cone of silence" phenomenon: nothing controversial can be spoken, problems cannot be acknowledged out loud. Anyone who attempts to raise a concern, challenge authority or tradition, or resolve a disagreement is silenced, often passively through being ignored, delayed or minimized.

Origins of the Peacemaker

Peacemakers often describe an early environment in which conflict was destructive, and was something to fear. You may have stepped into a role of being the one to try and keep the peace, or at least prevent the conflict from further escalation.

When you were the target of an adult's anger or disappointment, you learned to stay small, remain in the background, to avoid their attention. Keying off your parents' reactions, you may have internalized the message that your needs were a problem.

Whatever the specific circumstances that made your Peacemaker step forward, it will have provided you a love of peace and harmony, the capacity to reduce tension, and a selfless willingness to accommodate yourself to who others needed you to be.

When the Peacemaker is operating on your Inner Team without the balancing influence of the Warrior, you may experience:

• Difficulty knowing what you want

- Struggles with asserting yourself, particularly in situations where what you want or need might create conflict with someone else

- Withholding your contribution from a group, team or family, out of concern that it will create problems and disrupt relationship harmony.

- At the extreme, you may contort yourself to ensure you don't get into conflict with someone else, even when conflict is both healthy and necessary. For example, a spouse who denies the impact of their partner's drinking, or a leader who reassigns an underperforming employee to a new role rather than give her critical feedback.

CHAPTER 5

THE VULNERABLE CHILD

"Vulnerability is the birthplace of love, belonging, joy, courage, empathy, accountability, and authenticity. If we want greater clarity in our purpose or deeper and more meaningful spiritual lives, vulnerability is the path." – Brene Brown

---

Every human has a shared experience from their very earliest years: feeling helpless, wordless, dependent, and powerless to protect yourself. The imprint of these earliest experiences in childhood is carried by your Vulnerable Child.

This young part of you is a lifelong presence. No matter how resourceful and capable you become as an adult, the small, powerless, young part of remains eternally present within you.

The Vulnerable Child is the most common Outsider on the Inner Team. You turn away from this tender, sensitive, fearful part of who you are in an attempt to escape from the pain she carries. But when you cut yourself off from this part, not only do you lose access to her extraordinary gifts, but you also create the conditions for your Insiders to take over your Inner Team, each a part of a suit of armor you wear to guard against feeling vulnerable.

As you first become aware of the Vulnerable Child within, and then learn to relate to her with compassion and care, it opens the door to experiences that everyone craves: deep intimacy, unguarded trust, emotional vitality, and the capacity to be present to what is occurring in the moment.

Re-integration of the Vulnerable Child into the Inner Team is one of the most important objectives of Inner Team Dialogue, and simultaneously some of the most challenging inner work you can undertake.

EXERCISE: MEET YOUR VULNERABLE CHILD

Picture yourself as a young child, around age four.

- What do you look like? (*it can be helpful to look at an old photo to remind you*)
- What are you wearing?
- Where are you?
- Which adults are around? How about siblings? Friends? Pets?

Now imagine how your four-year-old self would have finished these sentences. Put yourself into the mind of a little child as you reflect, and keep your answers simple enough a four-year-old would understand them.

- It frightens me when...
- I really don't like...

- I get sad when…
- It makes me mad when…
- I get overwhelmed by…
- What makes me feel safe is…

THE WORLD OF THE VULNERABLE CHILD

"The cry we hear from deep in our hearts comes from the wounded child within." - Thich Nhat Hanh

The Vulnerable Child inhabits a world of fears, irresistible needs, and strong emotions. You're super sensitive to what's going on around you: when the grown-ups are upset, you get upset too. There are big, scary adults whom you don't understand, and a bigger, scarier world you don't know how to navigate. There are places and people in your world that feel safe, and other places and people that feel dangerous, and make you want to run away.

You rely on the grown-ups in your life for everything: food, shelter, comfort, guidance, safety, protection, and making meaning of the confusing, complex world you were born into.

Sometimes they come through for you, and attend to your needs, and you feel safe and loved. And sometimes they don't, and then you get even more frightened.

When it all gets too much, you don't have the words to express what you're feeling, so it bursts out of you as sadness, fear, or rage. You burst into tears at the slightest provocation, cling to Mom or Dad's legs, or run away to hide.

The Vulnerable Child feels every emotion intensely, particularly fear, in all its forms.

- Fear of **harm** (attacked, judged, shamed, humiliated, boundaries violated)
- Fear of **rejection** (abandoned, excluded, overlooked, dismissed, isolated)
- Fear of **manipulation** (controlled, betrayed, smothered, guilted)
- Fear of **failure** (missing the mark, not measuring up, failing to perform)
- Fear of **success** (unwanted attention, excessive demand, unworthiness)
- Fear of **irrelevance** (un-needed, disconnected, without value)
- Fear of **loss** (grief, disappointment)

The Vulnerable child can create a kind of boundary-less state in which no sensation, feeling or experience can be kept out, and everything gets through. In part because of this, the Vulnerable Child is prone to overwhelm – the feeling of being flooded with inputs you can't process, challenges that feel too much. It's a helpless feeling of being unable to cope, powerless to respond to what is being asked of you. It can feel like confusion or disorientation, in which you can't make sense of what's happening. Inarticulate frustration is also characteristic of the Vulnerable Child, the feeling of being unable to express in words what is felt or sensed, unable to name what is occurring. It is felt somatically, a whole body experience of "too much".

THE GIFTS OF THE VULNERABLE CHILD

Because our Vulnerable Child carries our pain and remembers our trauma, its gifts of empathy and intimacy are often overlooked.

Children love in a way that is simple and uncomplicated, generous and spontaneous. Young children have the capacity to make friends in an instant, because the Vulnerable Child can feel an instant connection without the need to build trust over time.

Because it is so open-hearted, undefended and without armor, the Vulnerable Child is the part of you which is most able to experience intimacy. When the Vulnerable Child feels safe, it will be possible to lower your guard, give and receive love freely. When the Vulnerable Child feels unsafe, this will not happen. Because of this, it is the character who most determines if not the overall success of intimate relationships, then certainly the degree of intimacy within them.

Because the Vulnerable Child is dependent on adults to meet its needs, it is extraordinarily sensitive to what other people are feeling, even experiencing other's emotions as your own. It's a major source of your empathy.

THE DANCE OF POWER AND VULNERABILITY

We live in a culture that celebrates and praises power, and demonizes vulnerability. In almost every area of society, vulnerability is not treated kindly. Think of the number of messages you've received over your life that celebrate empowerment, toughness, grit, or fearlessness. There are many contexts in which showing vulnerability will indeed make you a target, if not of violence, then certainly of rejection and ridicule.

The narrative of empowerment is everywhere. It's in the DNA of the personal growth industry. We are told that success is synonymous with capability, strength and toughness. It's a tremendously seductive narrative. Given the choice of feeling either powerful or powerless, which would you choose?

But it's a false binary. If you are only allowed to feel empowered, potent, capable and in charge, you will internalize the message that you must ruthlessly suppress any part of you that does not feel this way, from your grief to your confusion to your exhaustion. Whenever you do this, you are turning away from the Vulnerable Child within you, until you barely remember that it lives within you, and it becomes an Outsider on your Inner Team. In the short term, you feel less intensely afraid, but at a cost: intimacy and trust will disappear too.

How you manage the relationship between your power and your vulnerability will impact every area of your life. Because this is a polarity – a balance to find rather than a problem to solve – you cannot choose one over the other and thrive. Real strength comes from the capacity to hold both simultaneously, to be capable *and* incapable, powerful *and* powerless, tough *and* tender. Without the capacity to hold this tension, the only kind of power we can experience is very fragile indeed.

THE VULNERABLE CHILD OUTSIDER

When was the moment that you decided it wasn't safe to show your vulnerability?

I have a visceral memory of being eight years old, on the playing fields of a new school, crying after losing a game of football with my classmates. The boys in my class teased me so mercilessly that I made an internal decision never to let anyone see me cry, ever again. It was my first move in exiling my Vulnerable Child, in an effort to conform to the social pressure that men should be tough. My vulnerability remained inaccessible to me for years thereafter.

I happened to learn this lesson at school from the reactions of my peers, but it could just have well happened at home, where my sadness or fear could have been met by a parent who demanded I toughen up and get over it. Wherever the precipitating event (or trauma) related to showing vulnerability occurred, there was a moment when your Vulnerable Child became an Outsider. Sadly, there are few exceptions: no one gets through childhood with their heart unscathed.

This has devastating effects in every sphere of life, most notably on your capacity to trust other people. To trust is to share information that could be used against you, to open yourself up to being harmed. When you are unable to open yourself in this way, your communication with others inevitably becomes selective. You will curate which thoughts, feelings, needs or reactions you share, and which you keep hidden. Armored up against being hurt, your relationships will become more transactional, cool and distant, lacking intimacy and vitality.

When there is no permission to be tender, afraid or open, what remains is to show the world only those parts of you that are fearless, tough, untouchable. Think of someone who is lost but too stubborn to ask for directions, a phenomenon executive coach Kelly Dobson has dubbed the "advice-resistant personality".

The longer the Vulnerable Child has been an Outsider, the greater the concern that if you acknowledge what she's feeling, you'll become trapped in pain from which you will never escape. In a circular logic, the very fact of acknowledging that you have this vulnerable part inside you triggers feelings of vulnerability.

Your Inner Critic, tasked with protecting you from vulnerability, must guard against this at all costs, and will attempt to convince you that acknowledging those feelings to any degree is dangerous, something only wusses and snowflakes do.

THE COSTS OF DISCONNECTION
WITH VULNERABILITY

When you witness a loved one's pain, loss, confusion or wordless rage, how easy is it for you to be present? Can you be a compassionate witness to those feelings, or do you say something to make the other person "feel better," (that is, to make the difficult feelings go away)?

How you relate to your own Vulnerable Child will determine how you react when you glimpse vulnerability in others. If you can't be with your own Vulnerable Child, you may experience some of the following:

Rescuing: When faced with others' pain, you'll feel the urgent, even irresistible impulse to do something (anything!) to make those feelings go away. This looks like offering unsolicited advice, offering a consoling cup of tea, attempting to "fix" those negative emotions by wheeling out a comforting platitude or positive mantra. This fixes nothing, and runs the risk of leaving the other person feeling unseen, unheard, their vulnerability minimized or dismissed. This is not an argument against taking compassionate action to relieve the suffering of others, far from it. But when faced with suffering, however, it's important to pause to distinguish whose pain you are responding to: yours, or the other person's?

Risk blindness: Suppressing your Vulnerable Child's fear signals can blind you to genuine threats and risks, such as the early symptoms of an illness. You may minimize a threat, convincing yourself that a real danger is small, or the threat is a hoax, because facing it would require an encounter with your own vulnerability. When you cannot connect with the part of yourself that feels fear, you may appear outwardly fearless, but you will not have access to the crucial, sometimes life-saving information that fear provides about real dangers.

Toxic Positivity: If you cannot be with the part of yourself which feels hopeless, lost or powerless, labeling these as "negative" emotions, you are at risk of using positive thinking as a defense. Toxic positivity is the attempt to remain unconditionally positive when vulnerability is triggered. It denies the reality of pain and struggle, and refuses to acknowledge legitimate problems and difficulties. The word for this denial of someone else's pain is gaslighting.

Arrogance: If you cannot be with the part of yourself that is uncertain or confused, you may armor yourself with the certainty of being right. Any disconfirming data, which might produce vulnerable feelings of doubt, will be rejected. If you pretend you're right, you never have to feel the confusion and embarrassment when you realize you were, in fact, wrong.

Empathic misses: An empathic miss is a failure to recognize signals that someone else is frightened, in pain, or in need of help. When you miss the signals that someone really needs you to empathize and care, their vulnerable child will not feel safe with you. It will withdraw, and may not be willing to emerge in your presence again, without significant re-building of safety. An empathic miss can be the incident that breaks a relationship, sometimes beyond repair.

Lack of Courage: As Brene Brown has so clearly described through her research and teaching, there is no courage which does not require vulnerability. A life without courage will eventually become very small, because only those experiences which don't trigger vulnerability will be permitted. If you can't be with your Vulnerable Child, you are likely to remain trapped within your comfort zone, unwilling to feel the feelings involved in new experiences, initiating changes, or taking risks.

Vicious Inner Critic: When Vulnerable Child is disowned, its characteristic emotions of fear, sadness and confusion - if they are acknowledged at all - will be interpreted as signs of weakness. But because these feelings are unavoidable, they will be accompanied by fierce self-criticism and self-shaming, as the Inner Critic blares its warning that these feelings are incomparably dangerous.

THE GOOD PARENT: CARING FOR EACH OTHER'S VULNERABILITY

When you are fortunate enough to be with a partner who meets your vulnerability with compassion and acceptance, it feels amazing. Your Vulnerable Child, so long deprived of the kind of compassionate parenting it always wanted and needed, feels safe to emerge. In the presence of your lover, your Vulnerable Child feels seen, validated and accepted rather than ignored, judged and rejected. You feel safe to lower your guard and open up. Intimate connection emerges. You feel like a different – and better – person when you're around this amazing partner.

The Vulnerable Child in you connects to the "good parent" in your partner, and you begin to rely on them to care for your vulnerability. When they do so successfully, you feel safe and cared for. Many relationships operate by an unspoken agreement to create safety for each other's vulnerabilities. You recognize there are some behaviors in you that trigger your partner's vulnerability, and you love them enough that you decide to stop behaving that way. And they (hopefully) do the same for you. This can create a safe, positive partnership that can last for decades.

But there are side effects. When your partner is responsible for parenting the Vulnerable Child in you, the relationship will inevitably take on the quality of a parent-child bond. It will feel safe, but not passionate. You stop reacting to your partner's irritating actions and words, minimizing their importance. If you've ever told yourself to hide your anger with your partner's behaviors because he/she is a good person, or a good provider, or a good parent, you've experienced this pattern. As conflict in the relationship is suppressed, a progressive deadening of vitality follows.

The parts of yourself that your partner cannot be with don't go away, for all your efforts to suppress them. You become a slightly smaller version of yourself, wondering what happened to qualities you had before you entered this relationship, perhaps like flirtiness, or a willingness to take a risk. For many people, those parts that aren't permitted in their primary relationship will emerge outside it, with a person who <u>can</u> be with them, even celebrates them. This has led to countless crushes, attractions and affairs.

Even when it doesn't lead to an affair, your partner will inevitably be an imperfect parent to your Vulnerable Child. They will not always respond in the nurturing and compassionate way you desire, and you will feel betrayed. The relationship can go from safe and warm and to rejecting and distant, sometimes in an instant.

RELATIONSHIPS WHEN THE VULNERABLE CHILD IS PERMITTED

The solution is to cultivate your own "inner parent", who can provide what your Vulnerable Child most needs. The more this need is met from within, the more you can relieve your partner of this responsibility. This is what enables an intimate relationship to shift from a parent-child pattern based on dependency, to an adult-adult connection based on interdependence.

When you have access to your Vulnerable Child, you will be able to disclose your vulnerable feelings to your partner without a demand – spoken or unspoken – that they make you feel better. This emerges as a willingness to be more direct, authentic and clear with your partner: you can let them know how your Vulnerable Child reacted to their words or actions, without making them responsible for that impact.

Your Vulnerable Child needs you to be its compassionate witness. This is the job of the Inner Leader, because no character can do this.

THE INNER LEADER AS INNER PARENT

Every time your Vulnerable Child reacts to a perceived threat, one of your Insiders will be there in a millisecond with a response to keep you safe. This happens automatically, without conscious thought. But paradoxically, the more successful your Insider's strategy, the less the Vulnerable Child gets what it really needs, which is to be seen and heard, to receive a kind of compassionate inner parenting. You bounce off your vulnerability, and into your place of power, barely aware that there was a moment of pain, fear or loss.

So what does it look like to be an effective inner parent to this most tender, vulnerable part of who you are? It requires acknowledging and witnessing the vulnerability, rather than ignoring or suppressing it.

Reconnect to that picture you created of yourself at four years old. You're feeling sad and frightened. What is it you really want from the adults in your life, at that moment? What do you not want?

I'm guessing your answer includes some version of wanting to be listened to, to have your feelings validated with empathy and compassion. You don't want to be ignored, dismissed, fixed, or to have your experience minimized.

When your Inner Team's Insiders try to protect you from feeling the Vulnerable Child's pain, they are limited in what they can offer. Indulger can pour you a glass of wine to take the edge off. Pusher can distract you from your pain with a list of tasks that urgently need to be completed. Rational can take you out of your pain and into your intellect, with clever explanations of what caused the vulnerability. Spiritual can infer a higher meaning from what occurred.

All of these are kindly intended, but none can offer the "good parent" response of listening, empathy, calm, patience and compassionate presence. That's the job of the Inner Leader, operating as Inner Parent.

INNER PARENTING OF THE VULNERABLE CHILD

Parenting your Vulnerable Child involves three related actions: sense, witness and acknowledge.

Sense

When your Insiders activate, your Vulnerable Child was activated first. Acknowledge your Insiders' protective impulse, and reassure them that you, the Inner Leader, are in charge, and you can protect them. Ask if they would be willing to step back.

As your Insiders step back, you may become more aware of your Vulnerable Child's emotions, including sadness, fear, overwhelm or powerlessness. See if you can tune into where in your body you most feel the presence of your Vulnerable Child. Common locations include the lungs (shallow breaths), throat (a lump in the throat), chest (tightness), shoulders (raising, or rolling forward), or belly (tension in the solar plexus).

Witness

Whatever emotion or body sensation you notice, stay with it a little longer than you ordinarily would. Witness the sensation without trying to suppress it. Do not immediately try and "breathe through" it, relax your muscles, or do anything that makes the sensation reduce in intensity or go away altogether. Just notice the sensation, let yourself experience it. All the feels! If you can give yourself fully to the experience, emotions typically pass quite quickly. This is helped by breathing and movement. Let your whole body participate in the experience.

Acknowledge

Acknowledge the presence of your Vulnerable Child. Let her know that you see her sadness, anger or loss. Affirm her right to feel this way. Ask her what she needs you to know. Listen, and show her that you've heard her, you've registered her discomfort, and that you will keep her safety in mind.

If she needs to have a good, cathartic cry, don't shut her down or tell her to feel better. If you're not in a safe space to do so, ask her to pause, and promise you will return to witness her at a future moment that is more conducive.

WHEN TO GET HELP WITH LEARNING
TO BE AN INNER PARENT

If you are aware that your Vulnerable Child is still carrying the after-effects of trauma, seek professional support to help you through this experience safely. The best therapists and coaches can hold a compassionate, patient, non-judging Inner Leader

227

presence in relation to your Vulnerable Child. They serve as a role model for how to do this for yourself. If your real parents couldn't do this, there is enormous benefit from partnering with someone who can model what this looks like.

THE INSIDER VULNERABLE CHILD

The Vulnerable Child is typically an Outsider, but like any other character, it can be an Insider too. This happens when you start to identify with your vulnerable, powerless feelings. This identification with vulnerability produces two related characters: the Victim and the Hypochondriac.

The Victim makes the Vulnerable Child's experience of being powerless the defining truth of who you are. If you fully believe that life happens to you and you have no power or agency, then you cannot be held responsible. If you fully believe that you are completely dependent on others' care to survive, you will react angrily when they don't take the responsibility for you which you feel unable to take for yourself.

The Hypochondriac is similar, but experiences the vulnerability physically, as actual illness, or the perception of medical symptoms. This character wants to communicate how much they hurt, in the hope that their Vulnerable Child will be met with kindness and care.

Like other forms of vulnerability, neither the Victim nor the Hypochondriac are kindly treated. Both are attempting to get the needs of the Vulnerable Child met by eliciting care and attention from others. Viewed compassionately, their complaints and demands are best understood as a cry for help, and a lack of capacity to access characters that have a sense of power, agency and resourcefulness. They seek these in other people, making others responsible, which inevitably creates parent-child dynamics in the relationship.

CHAPTER 6

THE INNER CRITIC

This chapter explores:
- *What the Inner Critic is, and how to identify it*
- *How the Inner Critic is trying to protect you*
- *How the Inner Critic partners with Characters on your Inner Team*
- *What it takes to "defang" the Inner Critic*
- *Understanding the Critic as a signaling device*

The best-known character on the Inner Team is, without doubt, the Inner Critic. It's such an important character that it gets a chapter all to itself.

The Inner Critic goes by many names, including the super-ego, the saboteur, the gremlin, and memorably, *Brain Rats* (from the hilarious song of the same title by Barbara McAfee).

A quick Google search rapidly reveals an overwhelming consensus that the Inner Critic is *bad*, and will crater your self-esteem, confidence and efficacy. You'll find countless articles on managing, eliminating and taming your Critic, in order to control its pernicious influence in your life.

An unchecked Inner Critic can indeed create untold misery and suffering. No other character will be as hard on you. No other character is as determined to find you lacking, worthless and devoid of redeeming virtue.

But there are no bad characters on the Inner Team, and this applies to the Critic too. The Critic is trying to protect you, in the only ways it knows how, which happens to involve being harsh, judgmental and negative.

The Critic <u>feels</u> like your enemy, but it's best understood as an ally in heavy disguise. In this chapter, we're going to turn towards the Critic with curiosity, to reveal what it's really up to, and why it does what it does.

While getting rid of the Critic is neither possible nor desirable, it <u>is</u> possible to have the Critic participate in your Inner Team without causing suffering.

But before we talk about how this can occur, first we need to explore how to recognize the Critic.

RECOGNIZING THE CRITIC

The Inner Critic is a universal character. Everyone has one. It is an actively negative voice, providing a mean-spirited running commentary on you, reminding you of all the ways you're deficient, lacking, and not enough. For the Inner Critic, nothing you do measures up. You are fundamentally flawed.

If you succeed, it must have been luck. If you fail, it was because you deserved to, and it's amazing it didn't happen sooner. If others think highly of you, your Inner Critic will whisper, "If they only knew..." If others say mean things about you, it will confirm that these criticisms are completely valid, and it is inevitable that others will find out how fatally flawed you are.

The Inner Critic is the voice of the Judge, turned inward. Where the Judge focuses its attention on others and finds them wanting, the Inner Critic turns its attention on you. Not only will it always find you unsatisfactory, it has no interest in being fair and balanced in its assessment.

Shame, low self-confidence and impostor syndrome are the three clearest indicators of an active Inner Critic.

Here are some other ways to recognize the Critic:

Catastrophizing

The Critic articulates the worst-case scenario, catastrophizing even minor issues (*"The report had a spelling error, you're going to get fired."*). It whispers the least charitable interpretation of any situation, finding negative motives in the smallest observations (*"She frowned at me, she must want a divorce."*). And most of all, whatever the problem, is quick to conclude that you, and your many flaws, are the cause (*"If you weren't so impatient, none of this would have happened."*)

The Inner Critic speaks with a voice of certainty and authority, as if its catastrophic perspectives are obvious, self-evident truths. As one client recently put it, "My Critic doesn't speak to me, she hands me pronouncements carved on stone tablets."

You are Your Faults

When your Critic speaks about your work, it will keep reminding you of the most minor flaws and oversights, never strengths or successes. No amount of contradictory data will convince the Critic otherwise. Even if you come up with a compelling, even irrefutable argument to challenge your Critic's low opinion of you (*"But I made the sale!"*), it will simply change its angle of attack, hinting that perhaps you fooled them this time, but it can't last… because eventually they'll learn that you're not very smart.

The Critic is the master of deflecting attention away from strengths and successes. One of my clients, an engineer who's considered a luminary in his highly technical field, reported that his Critic would brush past his technical brilliance, and focus entirely on his challenges with interpersonal relationships. For the Critic, it's your failures that define you, regardless of your achievements.

What You Fear is True About You

The Critic targets whatever you most fear might be true about you. Whether it's focusing on the size of your hips or the size of your bank account, the options are too big or too small, never just right.

Anything society at large views as important, the Critic can turn against you. This is why weight, attractiveness, intelligence, power and status are magnets for Critic attacks. What's objectively true about each of these matters not at all: you could be a perfect weight, stunningly attractive, super smart, rich and powerful, and the Critic will still find avenues of attack that stoke doubt and uncertainty.

You need to be fixed

The Critic is often the character who prompts you to reach out to a coach or therapist, or enroll in a program that promises transformational change, in the hope that it will fix your faults, deficiencies and flaws. But when the Critic is in charge, no matter how much progress you make, you will feel no better about yourself, because the Critic will move the goalposts or refocus on the next problem. Paradoxically, Critics love personal growth programs, because any approach you might struggle to implement, or be imperfect at, offers yet more ammunition for an attack.

You need your Critic in order to Motivate You
One particularly slippery trick of the Critic is to make you believe that without it, you'd have no motivation to change (*"I'm hard on you, because otherwise you'd never get out of bed in the morning."*). They convince you that you need self-criticism to function, that shame is a powerful fuel for change. It's a kind of twisted logic, which can sound like, *"If you didn't hate your body, you'd never go to the gym."* The idea that you could love rather than shame yourself into change is completely foreign to the Critic.

THE PURPOSE OF A CRITIC'S ATTACKS

If you look under the surface of your Critic's attack, you'll quickly discover that it is not *randomly* vicious. There is a direct relationship between your Insider and Outsider characters, and the avenues of attack your Critic deploys.

As you learned in Chapter Two, your Insiders have rules of behavior that they believe will keep you safe. Break these rules, and you can expect an immediate reaction from your Critic, to let you know you're in danger. Its job is to keep your Insiders in charge, and to keep your Outsiders out.

It lives in a black and white world of good (your Insiders) and bad (your Outsiders), and it will police this tirelessly.

For example, if your Insider is the Pleaser, you stayed safe by attending to the needs of others, and ignoring your own. Your Critic's agenda is that you <u>never</u> break this rule. If you fail to meet others' needs, or (gasp!) attend to your own, the Critic will attack, accusing you of being selfish. The Critic won't gently remind you that being pleasing is the <u>right</u> way to be, it will yell that it's shameful to even contemplate setting a boundary or attending to your own needs, because only selfish people do that.

If the rule that kept you safe was to be clever and knowledgeable, then the Critic will shame you if you don't know the answer to a question, likely accusing you of being stupid.

If the rule was to always work hard, then the Critic will attack you for even considering taking a vacation or leaving your task list incomplete when you leave the office, declaring that it's proof you're irredeemably lazy.

You can think of the Critic as an enforcer. It doesn't have rules of its own, it enforces the rules of your Insiders. It doesn't matter to the Critic what the Insider's rule is, only that it's followed to the letter.

In practice, this means that the Inner Critic can appear quite different according to the Insiders who are running your Inner Team. Here are some examples of Critic phrases that emerge from its enforcement of particular Insider rules.

Pusher	The work isn't going to do itself. Just do it. Just one more before you quit. More is better. If you don't, someone else will. Want them to think you're lazy? You can sleep when you're dead.
Pleaser	You should have known. You'd better say yes. He won't love you unless... If you really cared... She's hurting, do something! You're so selfish.
Rational	Are you sure? An expert, you? There's so much you don't know. Prove it! You can't be certain. You're illogical.
Protector	It's too risky. It's going to fail. It's not worth it. You can't trust her.
Perfectionist	It's not right. Look it over one more time. You missed a spot. This isn't your best work. That was a mistake.
Independent	You shouldn't have trusted them. You could have done it better.
Special	You're boring. You're mediocre. They can't understand you. You're not like them.
Responsible	You're a flip flopper. No-one will trust you if you change your mind.
Rule Follower	You're going to get found out. You're going out looking like that?
Indulger	Better eat it now or there might not be any left.
Restrictor	If you eat that cookie, you won't stop. It's a slippery slope. You won't be able to control yourself.
Ordinary	Who are you to do that?
Competitor	He does it better than you, you're falling behind.
Spiritual	Some enlightened being you are!
Rebel	They're trying to control you. You're a sheep! A sell-out!
Warrior	You're going to let him get away with that? You're a wimp.
Loyalist	You're a quitter.

THE INNER CRITIC AS A SIGNALING DEVICE

Your Critic will not stop criticizing you when you stray from your Insider-driven behaviors. But it is possible to reach a point where your Critic's criticisms stop hurting.

The first step towards this is separation, the recognition that the Inner Critic is not you, simply a character on your Inner Team, doing its job the best way it knows how. There is a "you" which can observe the action of the Inner Critic, from the outside. This opens the door to observing the Inner Critic without needing to give the *content* of its criticisms any particular significance or importance.

The criticisms will still come, but stepping into the role of observer provides some much-needed distance from what your Critic wants you to believe, namely that its opinions are truths on which your survival depends. The Critic's certainty and intensity can make it sound like the voice of conscience. In reality, the criticisms themselves are no more than the Inner Critic following its programming in an attempt to keep you safe.

When you focus on the content of the Critic's attack, you can expect episodes of shame and self-loathing. When you focus on the Critic as a signaling device, the criticisms are merely data, which tell you which Insider's rule you broke, or are about to break.

When the shaming voice of the Critic appears, your job is to recognize it as a signal, and shift your attention to identifying which of your Insiders it is speaking for.

Here are some questions you can ask yourself when you first notice your Critic's activation:

- What did I do, think or contemplate, which triggered my Critic?
- If what I'm doing is bad, what does the Critic think is good? Which Insider character is the holder of this rule?

When your Critic attack was triggered by contemplating or acting on the prompting of an outsider:

- What are the Insider and the Critic afraid would happen if I connected with that opposite?
- What might be the gift of that opposite character, that the Critic and Insider don't know?

DEFANGING THE INNER CRITIC

Now you've recognized your Inner Critic for what it is: a signaling device, warning you of danger. It has no agenda except to keep you following the rules of your Insiders, and keeping away from the risks it associates with your Outsiders.

The moment you focus your attention on the <u>content</u> of its message, your Critic has the upper hand. You're fighting on its territory, arguing about who you should and shouldn't be, what you should and shouldn't do. Even if you attempt to disprove its criticisms with a counter-argument, you're still engaging with the Critic on its terms.

When the Inner Leader can observe rather than engage with the Critic, it becomes possible to respond in a way that breaks this cycle. A response that interrupts the cycle might sound like, "Hi Critic - thank you for the warning! I'm aware of the danger. And I've got it from here."

There's an inverse relationship between the Inner Critic and the Inner Leader. The more your Inner Leader takes on the responsibility for protecting you, the less the Critic needs to do so. One of the best indicators of the growth of your Inner Leader capacity is the reduction in frequency, intensity and duration of Inner Critic attacks.

How do you cultivate the Inner Leader? That's where we're going next in our exploration of the Inner Team.

PART 3
LEADING YOUR INNER TEAM

It is through realizing and trusting our capacity for a wise
and loving presence, through being that presence, that we
discover freedom from suffering. In the face of life's greatest
challenges, this timeless presence brings healing and peace
to our hearts, and to the hearts of others. The deepest
transformations... arise out a person's capacity to hold his
or her own inner life with a loving, wise awareness.

TARA BRACH (2012)

Now you have the framework and principles of Inner Team
Dialogue. You've been introduced to some of the characters which populate your Inner Team. While these are a
valuable source of self-awareness, awareness of characters
is insufficient to create meaningful, lasting change. The
source of deep change is always the Inner Leader.

CHAPTER 7

THE INNER LEADER

This chapter explores:

- *What the Inner Leader is and isn't*
- *How Inner Leader presence develops*
- *What the Inner Leader can do, which no character can*
- *How the Inner Team changes as the Inner Leader takes charge*
- *What becomes possible when the Inner Leader is in charge*
- *How to distinguish between Inner Leader and Characters*
- *Everyday practices to cultivate your Inner Leader*

Consider these two statements:

- "I am responsible."

- "A part of me is responsible."

The first is a statement of fixed, unchanging identity. Responsible is who you <u>are</u>, who you have always been, who you will always be.

The second statement acknowledges the responsible part, and allows the possibility that you might have other parts who <u>aren't</u> focused on being responsible.

And even more importantly, it also implies that there is a <u>you</u> which is observing the <u>part</u>.

This may sound like a small difference, but the separation between you, the observer, and the part being observed, is actually the central insight of all parts-work approaches. You can sum it up in a single statement: **you are not your characters.**

This is such a radical statement. Ask most people to describe themselves, and they'll use adjectives like helpful, creative, or driven. Each of these points directly at the qualities of their Insiders.

But if you're not your Insiders, then who are you?

Who you are is the Inner Leader, the observing, witnessing presence that allows you to notice the team of characters within.

If you're a bit confused right now, you're not alone. Visualizing characters is relatively easy: they have such distinct personalities that a picture usually comes quickly to mind. The Inner Leader is less tangible. You can think of it as a <u>process</u> of mindful, compassionate, appreciative observation. It's a way of being in relationship with your characters, conscious, attentive, accepting all, judging none.

HOW INNER LEADER PRESENCE DEVELOPS

The Inner Leader is cultivated through deliberate, intentional practice. It does not develop automatically. It's always a conscious decision to pay attention, to become aware of which character is prompting a thought or reaction.

With practice, it becomes less effortful to notice a particular character. The more times you notice it, the more familiar it becomes. The first encounter can feel like meeting a stranger, the second like encountering an acquaintance. Eventually, noticing a character within you will feel like recognizing an old friend, familiar and instantly recognizable.

The Inner Leader is a quality of presence you develop in relation to one character at a time. You can have complete awareness of one character and be completely blind to another. For example, you might instantly recognize your Rational character as you notice yourself thinking hard or analyzing evidence, and remain completely blind to the presence of its opposite, Feeling. Over time, you can train yourself to notice Feeling's intuitive impressions, empathic responses or sensitivity to changes in mood.

As your Inner Leader presence develops in relation to a character, you become more and more aware of how it operates within you. You'll be aware of both its gifts and its liabilities. One indicator of Inner Leader presence is a lack of defensiveness. Imagine someone commented that you can come across as cold or aloof: if you have a Rational Insider without Inner Leader presence, you might feel the impulse to defend yourself against this statement. With Inner Leader presence, there's an easy acknowledgment that yes, sometimes you can be a bit aloof.

Inner Leader presence is perhaps most evident in your ability to integrate both sides of a pair of opposite characters. As you develop awareness and appreciation of both sides, you'll find that it becomes easier to honor both. For example, if you have Inner Leader presence around both Pusher and Being, it will not be difficult for you to pause working through your task list to step back and reflect; it will also be natural for you to translate your reflections into actions.

You can think of Inner Leader presence as a kind of trusting relationship between you and your characters. The character trusts that you see it, understand it, and will neither ignore it nor misunderstand its intentions towards you.

The goal of Inner Team Dialogue is to cultivate Inner Leader presence in relationship with every pair of characters on your Inner Team. It's a process of becoming more conscious, so it's never finished. There's always more to learn.

That said, when you have developed a strong Inner Leader presence about one pair of characters, the next pair will become slightly easier. You become more comfortable with what it takes to hold the tension between opposites, and more attentive to the warning signs that you're taking sides.

As your Inner Leader presence grows to embrace a wider range of characters, a profound shift begins to occur. The Insiders who have run your personality for your whole life begin to relax their grip on your behavior, trusting that you, the Inner Leader, can truly lead the Inner Team. As the Insiders step back, their place is not automatically taken over by another Insider. The internal arguing, jostling and campaigning becomes less intense, less demanding. Calm begins to replace agitation and urgency.

In place of judgment, labeling, criticism and shaming comes something more appreciative, loving, curious, and inclusive. Internal Family Systems (which uses the term "Self" instead of Inner Leader), describes what it feels like when the Inner Leader is in charge using the "eight c's": *confidence, calmness, creativity, clarity, curiosity, courage, compassion, and connectedness.*

The Inner Leader Exercises Choice
While the Inner Leader is the observer of the Inner Team, it's far more than a passive, disinterested witness. The Inner Leader

actively chooses about when and to what degree to allow a character to influence your behavior.

It's the Inner Leader that can notice the impulse to take responsibility, for example, but not act on it. Inner Team Dialogue practitioner Ken Durbin offers a delightful metaphor for the Inner Leader's role: *"The engine is always running, but you don't have to put it in gear."*

A character makes choices like a judge, evaluating right and wrong, and opting for right. The Inner Leader makes choices like a mediator, listening to the needs and objectives of each side, generating dialogue, and seeking solutions that serve both sides. Characters tend to frame decisions as either/or, the Inner Leader as both/and.

WHAT THE INNER LEADER BRINGS TO YOUR LIFE

The Inner Leader's guiding principle is radical inclusiveness. Every character represents a valuable resource, all should be included.

I can't overstate how radical it is to include all the characters within you. Before the emergence of the Inner Leader, your identity formed around who you think you are (your Insiders) and who you think you are not (your Outsiders). As you begin to cultivate your Inner Leader presence, it becomes possible to re-integrate characters that you've previously rejected, to reclaim their gifts, to welcome and include their voice and influence on the Inner Team.

This requires real courage. For example, if you were raised to sacrifice your own needs to be of service to others (Pleaser), re-integrating a character that prioritizes your own needs

(Boundaried) can initially feel like a violation of your core values, because it seems selfish by comparison. The work of the Inner Leader is to appreciate the Outsider on its own terms, seeing it appreciatively, and setting aside former judgments.

Reintegration of these marginalized, underused Outsider characters can be very threatening to your Insiders. They will see their opposites as undermining all the ways they are trying to keep you safe. Your Inner Leader will need to reassure your previously dominant Insider characters that you're not abandoning them, and that you need their gifts as much as ever.

As your Inner Leader presence grows, you become more inwardly diverse. The reflex to judge a part of you as negative will soften and eventually recede, to be replaced with curiosity.

As this way of relating to yourself becomes more familiar, it begins to influence how you respond when you encounter people different than you in the outer world. Imagine bringing this curious perspective to someone of the opposite political tribe, or someone who comes from a culture with a radically different set of assumptions about the world.

As your capacity to embrace paradox and contradiction within you increases, so will your capacity to embrace it with your spouse, your kids, your workplace team, or any context that contains a diversity of opinion.

A VISION FOR THE INNER TEAM

As your Inner Leader presence grows, not only do you become more inwardly diverse and inclusive, your Inner Team becomes a resource rather than an obstacle to your worldly aspirations.

A high-performing Inner Team allows you to direct your energy toward achieving outcomes you care about, rather than endlessly re-litigating old internal battles about what is safe or virtuous. It brings with it a capacity to magnify the voices of the characters who have the resources you need. It brings the capacity to be truly at choice about how you act. Getting to this point is neither quick nor easy, but the impact can be transformative.

But while it can empower worldly achievement, the real contribution of the Inner Leader is best understood from a spiritual perspective.

Some religious traditions have promoted the belief that humans are basically sinful, and only by following that religion's rules of conduct can you emerge victorious over your baser instincts. You find echoes of this same foundational assumption in many psychological systems too, which detail how to "correct" faulty thinking (essentially, protective characters that they have judged and pathologized).

When people first hear about parts work, they often have a fear that if they turn towards their parts, they will discover something bad - possibly evil - within themselves. But this is the opposite of what people actually experience in parts-based coaching or therapy. As the characters' influence on your identity and behavior loosens, what emerges are not baser, more destructive, or more antisocial impulses. What emerges is an experience that who you really are, under the layers of conditioned and protective behavior, is a deeply compassionate, curious and loving presence.

My point here isn't to criticize religious dogma or psychological labels, but to contrast the lived experience of the Inner Leader with them. What if you trusted that who you are at your core, underneath the layers of self-protection and armor your characters have provided, is essentially loving? This assumption changes everything.

Whatever your religious convictions, I hope you share my feeling that the world could use more people who operate from love, compassion, inclusion and curiosity.

IS YOUR INNER LEADER IN CHARGE, OR A CHARACTER?

One of Dick Schwartz's insights about parts is that some mimic aspects of Inner Leader (called "Self" in IFS.) The Observer, for example, brings the capacity to pay close attention. Being provides a quality of calm, as do Minimizer and Peacemaker. The Artist brings creativity. Confident/Expert brings (you guessed it) confidence.

Each of these characters offers powerful gifts that <u>resemble</u> the Inner Leader, but they're not the Inner Leader. What all characters have in common, which is distinct from the Inner Leader, is that they insist on their preferred way of thinking, feeling or behaving, and warn against its opposite.

One of the ways to tell that you're operating from a character rather than the Inner Leader is the feeling of effort. There's always some energy going into holding back the opposite, like trying hard to stay curious when you notice judgment arise in you.

Inner Leader presence, by contrast, seems to emerge effortlessly as you develop a truly appreciative, inclusive relationship with both sides of a pair of opposite characters. As the influence of the characters recedes, Inner Leader presence is simply there, automatically and without striving.

When your Inner Leader is in charge, your experience of yourself is quite different than when you're being driven by one of your characters. Here are some differences which you may notice:

INNER LEADER	CHARACTER
Choice: you can be aware of a stimulus, even the impulse to react a certain way, but not act on it. You have the capacity to pause and choose.	**Automaticity**: you have an instant, automatic response to certain stimuli, which happens without your conscious choice.
Self-Compassion: You feel appreciative towards every part of who you are, grateful for its protection.	**Self-Judgment:** You judge certain thoughts, feelings, impulses and behaviors as negative. You want to stop them, even eliminate them altogether.
Flexibility: You're able to experiment with different ways of thinking, feeling and behaving.	**Autopilot:** You solve every problem with the same thinking and behaviors which have worked for you in the past.
Both/And: You can recognize contradictory impulses within you and seek solutions which honor both.	**Either/Or:** You recognize contradictory impulses and feel pressure to choose between them. You are prone to second-guessing the choice you made.
Nothing to Defend: You respond without defensiveness to other people's perceptions and judgments of you.	**Defensiveness:** You feel the need to defend who you are, to prove that a negative perception of you is incorrect.
Calmness: You maintain a calm presence, even as you notice emotions occurring within you.	**Reactivity:** You are easily triggered into strong reactions, which temporarily take over your behavior.

EVERYDAY PRACTICES TO CULTIVATE
YOUR INNER LEADER

The five "separation practices" listed below have a common purpose: to help you differentiate yourself from your characters.

1. Ask "Who?"

When examining your own thoughts, feelings or behavior, you can create separation between you (the Inner Leader) and your characters, by asking, "Who in me thinks that?" or "Who in me wants that?" Identifying a single character who's activated in you is helpful. When you identify two or more that have contrasting points of view, however, the Inner Leader starts to emerge naturally.

2. Use Parts Language

When you talk about your thoughts, feelings and inner experience, try changing your phrasing from "I'm feeling" to "A part of me is feeling..." Similarly, try changing "I want..." to "A part of me wants..." It may seem like a tiny difference, a matter of semantics, but it's not. Notice what happens when you use this kind of language. Many people find that it gently separates you from a thought or emotion, and makes room for other contrasting thoughts or emotions too.

3. Name it

Giving a part of you a name like "Warrior" or "Peacemaker" brings definition to this character's role on your Inner Team. It also means you can come back to explore the same part of you over and over again, deepening your understanding with each encounter. What name you choose for a character is unimportant, as long as you avoid pejorative labels, like Lazy or Selfish.

4. Visualize the character as a person

The more vividly you imagine a character as a real person, the more they'll come alive for you. Use the visualization prompts in the exercise in chapter nine. If you're artistically inclined, you can try to draw, paint or even sculpt them. Alternatively, try an online image search, or apply your mad AI skills to create a digital image that fits your imaginings.

5. Ask for advice

Your characters do not activate randomly: they do so to keep you safe. Invite them to share their advice: ask what they most want you to know or do.

6. Welcome it

This is disarmingly simple and powerful: once you've become aware of the presence of a character, give it a little internal nod of recognition, or a bow of respect. Show it you're aware of its presence. Always thank the character for showing up and protecting you, even if you choose not to act on its promptings.

CHAPTER 8

THE INNER LEADER
AND DECISION-MAKING

While Inner Leader presence affects every aspect of life, one of its areas of greatest impact is how you make decisions. In this chapter, we explore:

- *The role of your Insiders in your decision making*
- *When and how to consult your characters about a decision*
- *Decision remorse and the whiplash effect: what happens when a character isn't consulted*

I've been quite indecisive about what to include in this chapter about decision making.

A part of me (hi, Pleaser) is predicting your reaction, and suggesting I include what it believes will win your approval.

Another part really wants me to deliver the impression of unique expertise (thanks, Expert, and do I hear a little Special there too?)

My Perfectionist advises me, in the strongest possible terms, that I should immediately delete the sentences above, which it is convinced will undermine my credibility. Wouldn't it be the greatest act of hypocrisy to write a chapter on making decisions effectively, and then openly reveal your inner decision-making conflicts?

No, no it wouldn't.

Learning to make more confident decisions involves turning towards exactly these kinds of internal dialogues, getting curious about them, and listening to rather than judging or suppressing those voices. It's in the messiness of this process that real clarity can emerge.

If you're willing to acknowledge all of what you hear going on in your Inner Team's conversations, you might just find crucial information to inform the highest-stakes decisions you have to make.

MULTIPLE MINDS EQUALS INTELLIGENCE MULTIPLIED

"Neither of us has a fully functioning brain," my colleague Sarah declared, "and we shouldn't be let out alone. Together, we occasionally make sense."

Sarah and I are opposites. She is as quantitative, detail-oriented and structured as I am qualitative, non-linear and improvisational. She brings out rigor in my thinking, I bring out intuition in hers. Our professional partnership works, in an odd-couple kind of way.

The characters on your Inner Team are as different as Sarah and I. Each possesses a unique kind of intelligence, and is attuned to a certain kind of information. For example, Pleaser has an instinctive understanding of what others need, and how they'll respond. Perfectionist can identify flaws and errors that others might overlook. Protector can sniff out risks and threats that are invisible to other characters.

Each is a potentially crucial source of information when it comes to making decisions. And each can be as dumb as a bag of hammers when it tries to make decisions alone. Just like Sarah and I, no character is equipped to manage a consequential decision in isolation from its complementary parts.

A simple decision can be handled by a single character. Rational's logical and analytical approach, for example, is perfectly equipped to draw conclusions from quantitative data. Ask Rational to make a decision whether to end a relationship, however, and its limitations will become immediately apparent.

A complex, multi-faceted decision requires multiple points of view. The more points of view, the lower the risks of overlooking critical information, and the higher the chances of a well-thought-out decision. Imagine a business deciding to launch a new product with input only from Engineering, without consulting Sales, Marketing or Finance. The chances that decision will produce its desired outcome are slim.

The same principle applies to the Inner Team: all other factors being equal, a diverse and inclusive Inner Team will make better decisions than any single character.

Not only do multiple characters' points of view make your decision-making better informed, they also prevent second guessing. That forehead-slapping moment of regret that you didn't think of a factor sooner, is a sure sign that a character on your Inner Team should have been consulted earlier.

It's hardly a radical idea that entertaining multiple perspectives leads to better decisions, but in practice, it's hard to do. Your Insiders have been making your decisions for years. You're so familiar with their influence on your thinking that their decisions feel right and obvious, even when they're myopic.

What interrupts this cycle is the Inner Leader. This chapter outlines a method to invite your Insiders to step back and allow the Inner Leader to assume control of your decision-making.

This process doesn't magically make difficult decisions easy, stress-free and guaranteed to succeed. Taking on multiple points of view can initially make things <u>more</u> confusing. But considering more points of view is the key to making more confident decisions.

HOW YOUR INNER TEAM INFLUENCES THE DECISIONS YOU MAKE

Before we dive into the deep end of the decision-making pool, let's look at how your Insiders take charge of your everyday, low-stakes decisions.

LOW-STAKES DECISION MAKING: THE CLOSET EXERCISE

Try this exercise tomorrow, before you get dressed for the day.

1. Pick out an outfit, just as you normally would. *Don't overthink it... you can't do this wrong.*

2. Pause, and ask yourself what criteria you used to make the selection. Look beyond the obvious, such as weather conditions, to other factors, like what other people will think, or how a certain outfit makes you feel, or what you think the outfit says about you.

3. Which of your Insider character(s) might have prompted you to take those criteria into account in making this decision?

At the risk of stating the obvious, this exercise isn't about clothes. It's about becoming aware of how your Insiders already dictate the everyday decisions you make. Each uses different criteria, based on its own rules of what's most important.

For example, my Pleaser, who wants me to be liked, picks out clothes it thinks others will approve of. Pusher, which wants me to move fast, will have me choose non-binding workout clothes that don't restrict my movement. My Comfort Seeker chooses sweatpants, every single time. My Protector chooses clothes that are the most appropriate, to guard against the embarrassment of being either over or underdressed. My Perfectionist rejects, with a sneer, any clothes that have stains or wrinkles.

CLOSET EXERCISE, ROUND TWO
Hopefully, you've seen how some of your Insiders impact your decision-making when you're not paying attention. Now we're going to add another Inner Team partnering practice: Inviting

1. Choose a character on your Inner Team whom you know well. It doesn't matter which one you choose... whichever comes first to mind.

2. Take a moment to get connected with this character. Recall what it does for you, what it thinks is important, what rules it wants you to follow. Form a picture of this character in your imagination.

3. In your mind, invite the character to give you advice on what outfit you should wear today. Ask it to pick out an outfit that

it believes is the right one for you to wear today. Show it a few outfits, and see how it responds.

4. When it selects one, ask it why it chose that one. Listen to the answer.

5. Thank this character for its input.

What differences did you notice between how <u>this</u> character made the decision, and the decision you made by default?

You can repeat this with as many characters as you wish. If you feel moved to do so, you can act on the advice of one of them, and notice if it has any impact on how you feel as you wear that particular outfit today.

If you really want to have fun with the closet exercise, try inviting your Rebel, Princess or Flirty characters to pick out your outfit. Or for a contrast, your Conservative or Rule Follower characters. Unless your entire closet is comprised of only one color or style, they will definitely <u>not</u> pick out the same clothes!

If clothes aren't your thing, you can a variation of this exercise in other low-stakes decisions, such as:

- **Deciding on a meal:** who in you chooses off the menu in your favorite restaurant? Is it, perhaps, the character concerned with the price of the dish, with pleasure, with health, or with what others might think?

- **Deciding on a TV show:** invite a character to select a show to watch from your favorite streaming platform. Why that one?

- **Deciding a Route:** when driving between familiar start and end points, invite a character on your Inner Team to navigate. Before you start the car, ask them what they want to experience on this journey. See if you can come up with a route that makes this experience happen. If your Playful character navigates, you might take a <u>very</u> different route home, compared to the Responsible character's preference for the most direct route.

- **Deciding a Meeting Agenda:** who in you has an opinion on what items to discuss in a meeting at work? Experiment with following some of its advice.

These low-stakes decision exercises can be surprisingly liberating. When you have an Insider who's dominating your Inner Team, they will do everything to keep you on their own particular straight and narrow path, and life can get a bit predictable. For example, my Responsible character picked out all my clothes for years, which meant inexpensive and relatively conservative clothes that could be used for years in multiple settings. When I recognized this, I invited Playful to go shopping with me, and I came home with a bright purple shirt with a picture of an octopus riding a bike, which I absolutely love.

CHARACTERS' DECISION-MAKING CRITERIA

This table gives you a headline for how a selection of characters approach decision-making. Some characters aren't listed, because they don't demonstrate a distinctive decision-making approach. If you recognize a character operating in how you make decisions, you may wish to read more about that character in Chapter Four.

CHARACTER	MAKES DECISIONS BASED ON...
Artist	What is beautiful, allows the most room for self-expression.
Being	What produces a state of inward calm.
Boundaried	What meets your needs, and prevents others making decisions for you.
Comfort Seeker	What makes you feel most comfortable, right now
Competitor	What makes a win more achievable.
Controller	What gives you the most feeling of control, agency and autonomy.
Dependent	Whatever decision someone else makes for you.
Expert	What makes you feel most confident and certain.
Feeling	What your heart, intuition and gut says.
Improviser	What moves the story forward
Independent	What you can choose without needing external advice.
Indulger/ Spender	What offers pleasure and reward, right now
Learner	What you will learn the most from.
Messy	Whatever. It doesn't matter!
Ordinary	What doesn't draw any attention to you.
Peacemaker	What keeps the peace, minimizes tension.
Perfectionist	What avoids criticism.
Planner	What the plan calls for
Playful	What is the most fun.
Pleaser	What won't disappoint other people, and will earn their praise or approval.
Pragmatist	What is most functional and practical.
Protector	What's safest and lowest risk.
Pusher	What gets you into action soonest.

Rational	What you can justify with evidence, and prove to be right.
Rebel	What makes you feel most unencumbered and free.
Responsible	What duty and obligation require, what honors your commitments.
Rule Follower	What honors precedent and conventional wisdom.
Saver/Restrictor	What offers greatest rewards in future, no matter the current sacrifices.
Special	What expresses the uniqueness of who you are.
Thrill Seeker	What produces the most excitement and adventure, right now
Warrior	What challenges you, and honors your principles

ENGAGING YOUR INNER TEAM IN HIGH-STAKES DECISIONS

Unless you happen to be a fashion influencer, picking out an outfit from your closet is a pretty low-stakes decision. But what if it's a more consequential decision, like starting or ending a relationship or job? That's where you need to actively consult with your Inner Team, to gather information with which to make the best possible decision.

WHEN TO CONSULT YOUR INNER TEAM

The following are some indicators that actively consulting your Inner Team could be helpful:

- You are facing a complex decision with a non-obvious answer, where the range of possible outcomes is very wide.

- You are feeling anxious about what would happen if you make a poor choice.

- You are experiencing procrastination, delaying and deferring the decision.

- You are avoiding the decision altogether, despite knowing it must eventually be made.

- You are seeking counsel, advice and guidance from multiple people in your life, but not implementing their suggestions.

- You sense that your default way of making decisions might not fit the situation you are facing.

- You have framed the decision options in either/or terms, considering only two choices, but neither feels quite right.

- You are experiencing oscillation, going back and forward over the same ground, talking yourself into and out of each decision without being able to settle.

HOW TO CONSULT YOUR INNER TEAM

1. Start with your Insiders

As we've discussed, your Insiders have historically made your decisions for you. The way you're thinking about a current decision will almost certainly reflect what your Insiders think is most important.

Your first impulse in response to the decision you face will always come from your Insider. Your task is to recognize the Insider which is present, and how it may be influencing the way you're thinking about the decision. To understand how it's trying to protect you, ask:

- What decision do you want me to make?
- What makes this the right decision?
- What are you concerned will happen if I don't follow your advice?
- What rule of behavior do you want me to follow, to stay safe in this situation?

You can do this silently, in your head, or by journaling. The exercise is complete when you feel you fully understand why your Insider is advocating its preferred decision.

2. Solicit Input from an Opposite

The opposite character is the most likely to have the "answer" you've been looking for, to compensate for your Insider's blind spot. Getting to know this point of view follows a similar process to listening to your Insider:

- What concerns do you have about the Insider's preferred decision?
- What decision do you want me to make instead?
- What do you want me to pay attention to, that I might be ignoring?
- What makes this the right decision, from your point of view?
- What rule of behavior do you want me to follow, to stay safe in this situation?

As with the Insider exercise above, you can do this silently, in your head, or by journaling. The exercise is complete when you are aware of the potential downsides of your Insider's preferred decision, and you understand and appreciate the perspective of the opposite.

3. Test the Decision with your Inner Team

Once your decision is made, speak it out loud. Declare it like you mean it, and notice what happens in your body.

When your Inner Team is aligned around the decision, you're likely to feel calm, centered, neutral, peaceful. If you feel <u>anything</u> else, like a tightening in your chest, a slight headache, or a feeling or irritability or anxiety, there is another member of your Inner Team who isn't on board yet. If you're re-opening and relitigating the decision in your mind, someone on your Inner Team is saying no.

Return to step 2 above, and invite the character who is producing the sensation to share. Ask the character:

- What concerns do you have about this decision?
- What different decision would you prefer I made?
- What would need to change about the decision, or its implementation, in order for you to support it?

Let them know you want to hear what they have to say. You don't have to change your decision, but you do have to acknowledge the concerns. If you receive input which you think is valuable, adjust your plan accordingly.

CASE EXAMPLE: CONSULTING YOUR INNER TEAM ABOUT A CAREER CHANGE

Welcoming the voices of an opposite enhances your decision-making, and gives it the greatest chance of success. But some decisions are complex enough that they genuinely require more than two opinions. Brian's story is a case in point.

Brian was outwardly successful but increasingly bored. After fifteen years in corporate finance, the challenge had largely disappeared, and it felt like a grind. He applied for new jobs, but realized that doing the same job in a different organization wasn't going to scratch the itch. He told himself it was just a phase, trying to convince himself that his allergy to spreadsheets would pass. But it didn't.

Brian knew he wanted something more adventurous and less predictable than finance. He wanted work he cared about. His great passion in life was cycling, so it was unsurprising when his attention was captured by the opportunity to buy into a franchise that provided a mobile, van-based bike repair service. Brian did his due diligence, studied financials, evaluated competitors and reached the conclusion that it was a solid opportunity. He was thrilled to see a way forward that would allow him to leave cubicles and spreadsheets behind, work with his hands, hang out with cyclists, and make a decent living.

He excitedly shared the opportunity with his wife. Delighted to see the return of Brian's enthusiasm, she encouraged him to go for it. With financing approved and the franchise paperwork in hand, all that remained was to sign the forms to launch this new, exciting chapter of his career.

But he couldn't make himself sign. He did not give notice at his job. Brian was stuck, talking himself into and out of the decision, and he had no idea why.

It was at this point Brian hired me as a coach, to help him figure out what was going on, so he could get over whatever the barrier was. He described feeling paralyzed, and was beating himself up for what he saw as a failure of courage, expressing a fear that he wasn't cut out to be an entrepreneur.

I introduced Brian to the idea of the Inner Team, and explained that I was hearing a part of him which wanted to make the leap, and another part that didn't. He acknowledged that this was indeed the case. I asked him if he'd like to get to know those two parts of him a bit better, and he readily agreed.

Two characters emerged. First, a Responsible character who insisted that before he make a commitment, he needed to be 100% sure that he could keep it.

Second, a Playful character who was desperate to escape the corporate doldrums and do something exciting, new and adventurous. It reminded him that he only had one life to live, and he should have as much fun as possible, and enjoy the journey.

Playful was hitting the gas on Brian's career change, and Responsible was hitting the brake.

I asked Brian's Responsible part what it would take for it to support Brian's decision, and it had a surprising answer. It wasn't concerned about Brian's ability to make the bike repair business financially successful. It was concerned that his enthusiasm for doing work he loved would lead him to overcommit, overwork, to the point where he wouldn't be there for his wife and young son.

This completely reframed the problem. Brian and his wife started talking about how to draw boundaries around the work to limit both the number of hours he would spend, and the size of the geography he would cover. He created a list of criteria for what he would say yes to, and what he would decline.

As soon as these agreements were in place, Brian's hesitancy to sign the paperwork shifted into eagerness. The next day, he texted me two pictures: a photograph of the signed contract to buy into the franchise, and a screenshot of his letter of resignation.

Responsible was willing to support his career change because it was comfortable with the financial decision. Playful supported it because it would connect to his lifelong passion. The missing piece was the involvement of Boundaried, whose ability to set clear limits on his people-pleasing tendencies was crucial to Brian achieving a sustainable work-life balance.

Some months later, with his mobile bike repair business growing well, Brian told me the rest of the story. He was the eldest sibling of four, who had to take on a lot of responsibility early in life because his mom was chronically ill. The Responsible character in him had developed to help him bear the load of household obligations, while a Pleaser character had developed to help him put others needs before his own. The only escape he had from the heavy weight of responsibility was when he could ride his bike to school. Brian explained that his boundaried character had never developed, because his family was so genuinely in need of his help that he couldn't say no.

PREVENTING THE WHIPLASH EFFECT

Whiplash occurs after you've made a decision, and experience a forehead-slapping moment of regret, in which you ask yourself, *What the hell was I thinking?*

Whiplash is produced by a member of your Inner Team who was overridden or not consulted about the decision you made, and is now letting you know that you really should have listened to them.

For example, perhaps you impulsively bought a snazzy but expensive new outfit, only to regret it the next day when you realized your rent was due. That decision might have been made by Playful, but its opposite, Responsible, wasn't consulted, and now wants a serious word with you.

YOUR EXPERIENCES WITH WHIPLASH

Reflect on a decision you made in the past, which seemed like a good idea at the time, but you later came to regret. For the purpose of this exercise, don't focus on decisions that had negative outcomes that couldn't have been foreseen, such as a vacation ruined by bad weather or illness.

- What was the decision?

- Which member(s) of your Inner Team drove that decision?

- What did you later regret about the decision?

- Which member of your Inner Team might have been the source of that regret? What do they think you should have done instead?

Example:

- *I purchased a new outfit on impulse, the day before rent was due.*

- *The decision was made by Playful, because I was being spontaneous.*

- *I regretted my impulsiveness and short-term thinking.*
- *The character behind that regret was Responsible.*
- *My Responsible character told me that I should have thought more about my existing financial obligations.*

Whiplash experiences aren't fun. They're a fertile feeding ground for your Inner Critic, who will show up as an enforcer of your Insider, attacking you for the obvious folly of breaking the Insider's rules of behavior, or not following its approach to decision-making. The Critic will often pile on, concluding that your bad decision is definitive proof of your worthlessness.

A WHIPLASH TALE

Here's an example of a recent decision I made, only to experience whiplash soon after.

I received a Friday afternoon text from a friend, asking me to join him on a bike ride the next morning. He suggested we ride up a particularly steep mountain pass together.

I was exhausted after a long working week, and wanted a weekend of rest. Nevertheless, I felt pressure to say yes, even though I didn't really want to go.

Pleaser is one of my Insiders, and he routinely focuses my attention on others' needs, which seem way more important than my own. If my Pleaser is in charge of my decision-making, I make choices that I think others will approve of. I often find myself saying "Yes!" when I really mean "No!"

Pleaser's opposite – Boundaried – is a character I've been

working to integrate more. This is the part that reminds me that it's okay to ask for what I want, focus on my own needs, and say no when needed.

On this particular occasion, I didn't follow my Pleaser's advice, and declined my friend's invitation. I was initially proud of myself for keeping my Pleaser in check, and acting in a way that honored my need for rest. My friend would understand.

But seconds after I'd hit send on the text saying no, I started to worry. Would he be disappointed? Would he invite me next time he wanted to go for a ride? Had I just permanently damaged our friendship?

This was my Pleaser, reasserting his rules. My Pleaser believes that setting boundaries harms relationships. The right thing to do is accommodate yourself to others. I had focused on my own needs and said no, which broke my Pleaser's rule of behavior. There was a moment of vulnerability, the fear of being abandoned and rejected. And my Pleaser, whose role is to protect this particular vulnerability, reactivated to get me safely away from that feared outcome.

I found myself texting a second message, reversing my response. If he didn't have anyone else to ride with tomorrow, I asked that he let me know.

My version of Pleaser-Boundaried whiplash is to set a boundary and then walk it back.

As I reflected on what had happened, I realized I'd swung too far to the opposite: Boundaried had made my decision, and Pleaser hadn't been consulted.

What would have worked better, and perhaps prevented the whiplash, is this:

- I recognize the impulse to say yes to my friend's request, which comes from my Pleaser.

- I turn towards the Pleaser in me and ask it why saying yes is important. I listen to his point of view. My Pleaser tells me that it's important that I don't disappoint a friend.

- I acknowledge this point of view, and thank the Pleaser for his input. I offer a little bow of gratitude for helping me recognize what's at stake.

- I ask Pleaser if he's okay with me consulting Boundaried.

- I consult Boundaried, which helps me get clear about what I need, and what I will and won't do.

- I develop a solution that honors both: I text my friend that I'd love to ride, and propose another time because I'm too tired to enjoy it this weekend.

Listening to the Insider's perspective does not mean you are obligated to agree with them, nor act upon their advice. As the Inner Leader, it's your prerogative to choose a different path.

CHAPTER 9

EXERCISES, REFLECTIONS AND JOURNALING PROMPTS

Each of the reflections, exercises and journaling prompts which follows can help you get to know your Inner Team, build your Inner Leader presence, and partner effectively with your characters.

EXERCISE 1: EXPANDING YOUR VIEW OF YOURSELF

Exercise Purpose: To expand your understanding of who you are, by challenging the "monomind" assumption that you have a single, consistent personality.

1. What do you know, for sure, is true about your personality? Make a list of traits, behaviors, attitudes, ways of being in the world which are characteristic of who you are.

2. Think of a specific situation when you behaved in a way that was "out of character"? What behaviors, attitudes or traits were evident then?

3. In what situations do your behavior and thinking patterns change? (For example, when you're on vacation, or you're experiencing a period of stress.) What aspects of your personality become visible at these times?

4. Consider the people in your life who bring out a different side of you. For example, people who bring out your playful side, or your creative side, or your serious side. What aspects of your personality become evident when you're with them?

5. Consider qualities of your personality that were once accurate descriptors of you, but which don't seem to be true anymore. Can you find examples of situations where these older patterns emerged again, even briefly?

Look back over your responses to the reflections above. What if all these traits were "the real you"? What would it be like if you expanded your definition of your personality to include every trait, behavior, attitude and mindset you just listed, regardless of the frequency with which they make themselves evident?

EXERCISE 2: NOTICING CHANGES IN YOUR INNER TEAM

Exercise Purpose: To bring your attention to what experiences activate the characters on your Inner Team.

For this exercise, focus your attention on the thoughts, feelings, behaviors, sensations and beliefs that emerge within you, which are signals of character activation. It's not necessary to identify *which* character has activated.

1. Pick a period of time this week to observe your Inner Team. It's often easiest to notice character activation in

a specific situation that you anticipate being stressful or vulnerable (something like a first date, or an important meeting at work).

2. At the start of the period of time you've chosen, take a moment to register your "baseline" state. Notice the thoughts you're thinking, the emotions you're feeling, and any body sensations you're experiencing.

3. As you go through the time period you selected, see if you can notice when any of these <u>change</u>: for example, your thinking shifts, your mood changes, or you feel different in your body. Not every passing thought, feeling or body sensation is an indicator of a character's activation, but when your response feels very <u>familiar,</u> it probably is.

4. See if you can identify what occurred <u>immediately before</u> this change. (Hint: it's often a moment of vulnerability, often fear. For example, did someone praise or criticize you, or respond in a way you didn't understand? Did you face circumstances you hadn't anticipated or prepared for?)

EXERCISE 3: THE DELETE BUTTON

Exercise Purpose: Get curious about the judgments you make of certain parts of yourself, and learn to identify their source.

If you had a delete button that would permanently erase one of your patterns of behavior, which would you most want to get rid of? Try completing one or more of these sentence stems:

• I wish I was less ____

- I wish I could stop being so _____
- I wish I could get rid of my tendency to _____
- I wish I could break my bad habit of _____

The judgment that some part of you is bad and should be removed altogether <u>always</u> comes from another character in you. Let's see if we can identify the character which is the source of the judgment.

- If this is the wrong/bad way to be, what is the right/good way to be instead?
- What character advocates this as the right/good way to be?

You've just identified a conflict within your Inner Team, between the character who's behind the "bad" habit, and the character that thinks it knows a better way.

- *Reflect on the "bad" habit you identified above. Even if it is causing some problems in your life, try thinking of that habit as an attempt to protect yourself from a threat. Journal on how that habit protects you. See if you can identify any gifts, strengths or capacities it brings you.*
- *Notice how you feel towards this character after identifying its protective role, and the strengths it offers you.*

Example:
I wish I could get rid of my habit of trying to rescue other people by taking on their tasks as my own. A better way to be is to let people solve their own problems, and set clearer boundaries

about what I will and won't do. My rescuing pattern protects me from feeling powerless in the face of others' suffering. It's also how I earn the right to belong, by being helpful and needed.

The part of me which rescues is also caring and generous. It's the source of my empathy.

EXERCISE 4: GETTING TO KNOW YOUR INNER CRITIC
Exercise Purpose: Recognize your Inner Critic as a signaling device, indicating when you have broken a rule of behavior set by one of your Insiders.

You'll notice your Inner Critic activating through self-critical thoughts, harsh judgments of yourself, catastrophizing, ruminating, and a sense of worthlessness (see Chapter Six for more details). When these occur, shift your attention to the content of its criticisms:

- What are some of the things your Critic says are wrong with you?

- What "mistake" do you find it hardest to forgive yourself for? (For example, not being sufficiently empathic, or disciplined, or sounding uninformed)

- What does your Inner Critic turn into a crime? What does it want you to believe are wrong, bad or sinful ways to think, feel or be? (For example, you should never be angry, or self-ish, or be a burden on others).

Look back over your Critic's list of forbidden "criminal" behaviors.

- If these are the <u>wrong</u> ways to be, what are the <u>right</u> ways?

List these below as rules of behavior, using the sentence stems, "I should always…" and "I should never…"

These are the rules which kept you safe in the past. Your Critic wants to make sure you don't break them in the present.

EXERCISE 5:
CHARACTER ACTIVATIONS:
SOME JOURNALING PROMPTS

Exercise Purpose: These prompts are designed deepen your reflection about characters that activate on your Inner Team, so you can get to know them and understand their protective intentions.

When you notice an internal argument

The conversations, debates and internal arguments you have with yourself are typically between two or more characters. Often there's a cautious voice which says "Stop," and a more adventurous voice that says "Go!"

- *What were the two (or more) points of view in a recent argument you had with yourself?*

When you notice repeating thoughts

Characters reveal themselves in <u>repeated</u> thoughts. For example, if the thought "Why is this taking so long?" regularly passes through your mind, you might be experiencing a character who wants you to move fast. If you regularly find yourself thinking, "He's an idiot!" you might be experiencing a part that values intelligence.

- *What words or phrases do you say to yourself over and over again?*

- *What advice do you consistently give yourself?*

- *What rules of behavior can you identify in these repeating thoughts?*

When you notice rapid mood shifts
What to notice: Sudden shifts mood or feelings, rather than an inner dialogue in words. For example, a sudden change in mood like feeling suddenly hopeless, angry, sad or defeated.

- *What's an emotion that regularly arises in you <u>without an obvious external cause</u>?*

When you can't seem to interrupt a habit
Repeating patterns of behavior, particularly those you find difficult to stop, often indicate the activation of a character on your Inner Team. For example, a habit of reaching for a snack when you're anxious, or compulsively checking your phone.

- *Which of your habits of behavior would you find it hardest and most uncomfortable to stop?*

- *How does this habit protect you? What bad, difficult or painful feeling might you have to deal with if this character wasn't around?*

When you notice "autopilot" reactions
Notice what you do without thinking, the actions you take which seem to have no pause between stimulus and response. When you've acted without conscious thought, chances are

there's a protective character on your Inner Team who initiated that reaction. (For example, reflexively correcting an inaccurate statement, defending yourself when criticized, or silencing yourself when you disagree with someone.)

- *Which of your reactions are so automatic, they happen before you notice?*

- *If you could pause this reaction and choose how you'd like to respond, what would you do instead?*

When you notice judgmental thoughts
When you notice yourself passing judgment on someone else's behavior, whether critical or approving, you can be pretty certain these arise from a character on your Inner Team. For example, if you judge someone for being selfish, you're hearing the core belief of a character in your Inner Team who thinks the right way to be is selfless. Positive judgments work the same way too: judging someone else's behavior as exemplary or ideal also comes from a character.

- *What's a quality you judge negatively in other people? (For example, rudeness, or arrogance, or passivity). If this is the wrong way to be, what's the right way?*

- *What's a quality you judge positively in other people you respect or see as ideal? For example, kindness, or generosity.*

EXERCISE 6: VISUALIZING A CHARACTER AS A PERSON
Exercise Purpose: Engage your visual imagination to help you see your characters as people.

Your imagination is a wonderful ally in getting to know the characters who populate your Inner Team. This exercise works best for characters who are very active within you (your Insiders), but you can try it for Outsiders too.

- Think back to a recent time when a character within you was activated, ideally in the last week. Write down the thoughts and feelings that were present in you when this happened. Describe what that character activation felt like in your body. List any actions you took (or contemplated taking) at the prompting of this character.

- Now imagine: if these thoughts, feelings and behaviors were a person, what would that person be like? The following prompts can help you create a detailed visual impression:

  o What do they look like? (Tall or short? Younger or older? Facial expression?)

  o What clothes are they wearing? What colors are they? How formal or informal?

  o What is their posture like? Do they stand tall, or hunch over?

  o Do they have a scent?

- Let your imagination place the character in a setting. Let your imagination select a place that reflects who this character is.

  o Did you imagine them indoors or out? Is the space bright or dark? Spacious or crowded? What else do you notice about their environment?

- Invite the character to speak. What is their tone of voice like? Do they speak fast, or slow? Do they have an accent? Who do they sound like?

Now that you have created a vivid picture of one of your characters as a person, imagine yourself walking up to them. Visualize yourself greeting the character warmly. Explain that you'd like to interview them to get to know them better. You want to take a walk in their shoes. You have no agenda to change them or evaluate them, just to understand their world. Ask each of the following questions in your mind and listen for a response, or write down what they say in your journal.

- What's your role in my life?

- What are you trying to protect me from?

- If you weren't around, what bad thing do you believe would happen?

- What do you wish I knew about you?

Show them you've heard them. Before you end this encounter, thank them in whatever way feels right to you.

Notice how you feel towards this character within.

EXERCISE 8: BRING A CHARACTER AS YOUR INVISIBLE "PLUS ONE"

Purpose: Practice actively inviting a character on your Inner Team to step forward, and support you as you take on a particular task.

For example, imagine you're going to a party, and you're hoping to have a fun time. You invite Playful to join you, connecting with the character as you dress for the evening ahead, and letting him know that you want him to guide you.

Choose your ally:

- Pick an event that is coming up in the near future that you anticipate being uncomfortable or challenging, perhaps one you feel ambivalent about attending.
- Imagine this event going really well. What would happen, or not happen? What would the experience be like for you?
- How will you need to show up, to maximize the chances that it goes this way? What part of yourself will you need to draw upon? Which character on your Inner Team could be a valuable ally in making this happen?

Engage your ally as an active partner:

- Before the event begins, spend a few minutes alone, actively reconnecting with this character. Bring them into your mind as vividly as possible. You may wish to read the profile of the character from the Field Guide, to refresh your memory.
    - o Recall what it feels like when this part of you is active. Focus particularly on the feeling in your body.
    - o Recall this character's rules of behavior, how it wants you to engage with the world.
    - o Visualize them (the prompts from Exercise 6 can be helpful).
- Reach out to this character, and ask them to partner with you for this event.
- Show them you value and appreciate what they can bring you.
- Ask this character for one piece of advice about this event.
- During the event, keep this character in your mind. Feel its presence in your body.
- After the event, thank the character for its support.

CHAPTER 10

A VISION OF RADICAL INCLUSION

Join me for a brief walk in the shoes of an outsider to mainstream society.

You are an outsider. Perhaps it's your socio-economic status, gender identity or sexuality that others you. Perhaps you have a criminal history, medical history, or addiction history that sets you apart from the mainstream. Perhaps you have a visible or invisible disability.

Whatever the source, you have a story that is uniquely yours, a perfectly human story of heartbreak, trauma, joy, connection, loss, bravery and confusion.

But rather than having your story met with empathy or curiosity, the automatic reaction you receive from people in mainstream society is judgment. You are excluded, marginalized, and labeled, sometimes intentionally, sometimes by privileged indifference. You are "other". You are "them".

Now imagine someone approached you not with fear and judgment, but with curiosity. <u>What would it feel like to finally tell your story to someone who wants to hear it?</u>

This is what your Outsider characters feel like. They have a story to tell, and are desperately hoping you'll ask them to tell it, and that you'll stay connected with them. All the dynamics of inclusion and exclusion in society are reflected in our internal society, the Inner Team.

Insiders operate like a person of privilege in mainstream culture, whose voice is magnified. They look at Outsiders and judge them dangerous, and unworthy of love. They label, marginalize and exile.

When you shift your identification from your Insiders to the Inner Leader, the picture radically changes. The Inner Leader's appreciative and compassionate perspective embraces the other as unique and precious, possessing a unique point of view, distinctive gifts, their own story to tell.

Integrating your Outsiders expands your capacity, broadens your perspective, and helps you become a more whole, integrated version of yourself. But beyond these personal benefits, it sets in motion a process that can be genuinely transformative in relationships.

As you learn to be with the Outsider in yourself, you cultivate the capacity to be with differences without judging, labeling or rejecting them. This translates, naturally and effortlessly, into an accepting way of relating to others. Embracing your inner diversity, unconditionally, makes it possible to embrace outer diversity. Inner inclusiveness is the foundation of outer inclusiveness.

"Othering" is the source of so much unnecessary suffering. The solution to othering is inclusion. The solution to inclusion is the Inner Leader.

For all the practical benefits of a diverse, inclusive Inner Team, the goal of integration is fundamentally a spiritual objective. It's about coming home to who you have always been, as you release your hold on who you thought you had to be.

—*Paul Wyman, March 2024*

HOW WRITING A BOOK ABOUT THE INNER TEAM TAUGHT ME HOW MY INNER TEAM REALLY WORKS

THE GRAVEYARD OF UNFINISHED MANUSCRIPTS

Impossibly out of reach is how completing a book felt to me when I embarked on this project.

My track record as a writer was nine books started, none finished. Each time, I'd begin with enthusiasm, only to lose focus, motivation, and confidence, throw my hands in the air and give up. Like many people, I believed I had a book in me, but I didn't quite know how to get it out.

The fact that you're reading this book now means that I found a way past the obstacles that had stopped me before. The story of how that happened is the story of Inner Team Dialogue. Without the framework and tools of this approach, I'm certain this book would have been the tenth entry in my writer's hall of shame.

Writing a book – like any out-of-your-comfort-zone endeavor- is a fantastic way to activate your Inner Team. More than any other experience, this project taught me how my Inner Team really works, and what it takes to have your Inner Team support your aspirations and goals.

Knowing that the coaches who were learning ITD needed a comprehensive guide to the ITD body of knowledge, I launched into this project in late 2021 with excitement and boundless optimism. I was able to indulge my long-standing fascination with the material and draw on experiences with hundreds of coaching clients over two decades of practice. This produced a burst of creativity unlike any I'd experienced before. Words simply flowed onto the page. I had no idea how much I had to say on the topic. For the first time ever, writing felt easy.

I wish I could tell you that I rode this wave of creative energy all the way to submitting a finished manuscript to my editor.

The more I wrote, and the more deeply I engaged with this material, the more anxiety I felt. I began to question the purpose of what I was writing, to doubt my assertions, to second guess myself. What started as a torrent of words became a trickle, and eventually dried up altogether. Staring at my blank computer screen, I felt that dreadful sinking feeling of "Oh, no, not again!" I could see the road ahead. This book was heading to the unfinished manuscript graveyard to join its nine elder siblings.

The more I wrote about the Inner Team, the louder the conversation within me became. The price of writing about the Inner Team, it seemed, was a close encounter with my own.

Here's a glimpse of my conversation with myself:

Who are you to offer yourself as an expert?

As I tried to describe the way the Inner Team worked, I was increasingly aware of the many gaps in my knowledge. I ruminated on being asked a question I hadn't considered, and the searing vulnerability of being unable to answer it. What if my work contained a massive blind spot?

I tried to reassure myself that the ideas behind ITD were both solid and useful, reflecting on the many stories my students shared with me about using this approach successfully with their clients. But the fear of being exposed remained in the pit of my stomach.

Your writing sucks!

This missive from my Inner Critic shifted my attention from worrying about the ideas themselves to the deficiencies in my writing. I began to edit as I went along, rewriting paragraphs and chapters over and over again, hacking sentences apart, and recombining them in a thousand ways until I completely lost touch with what I was trying to say. My confidence in my writing ability drained away to nothing. The unfinished manuscript graveyard seemed like the proper place for the garbage I was producing.

You're lazy! Sit your ass down and finish the goddamn book!

As my writing output slowed and dried up, I found myself thinking that the root cause was, in fact, laziness. I wasn't trying hard enough.

Determined to prove that I wasn't lazy, I pushed myself harder and harder. The added pressure did nothing to help my creative flow, and the accusation of laziness got louder with every unproductive writing session.

The thought that I wasn't trying hard enough woke me at 2.30 a.m. one morning. Determined to give every ounce of effort I had within me, I dragged myself out of bed, and was soon sitting in my dark office, staring at the bright, blank computer screen.

I was a tangled mess of confusion, doubt, fear, and self-hatred. Tears rolled down my cheeks. I was an ignorant, talentless, lazy hack. The blank screen proved it.

Just give up, the voice said.

"Who in you thinks that?"

The urge to give up was becoming harder and harder to resist. But I didn't want to walk away from yet another unfinished manuscript, and the accompanying stink of failure and unfulfilled potential.

So I called a friend. As I shared my turmoil, she asked me the question I'd asked others a thousand times: "Who in you is thinking these thoughts?"

I was momentarily overcome with embarrassment that I could teach this work but utterly forget to apply it to myself. As Richard Bach said, you teach best what you most need to learn.

A CLOSE ENCOUNTER WITH MY INNER CRITIC

As the embarrassment faded, her question offered me a lifeline. It allowed me to shift from being the thinker of these thoughts to the observer of them. What was immediately clear was that my Inner Critic had activated the moment I ventured out of my comfort zone into the unfamiliar territory of being an author.

According to my critic, this could only reveal my many deficiencies, so it did everything in its power to convince me that I was not up to the perilous task of writing and publishing the book.

Naming this as the Inner Critic's voice was useful, but insufficient. It still yammered away whenever I sat down to write. While my impulse was to try and ignore it, I knew that defanging my Critic would require turning towards it with curiosity. It attacked three deficiencies:

- Not working hard enough, or producing enough
- Not being knowledgeable enough
- Not writing with perfect clarity

If these were the bad, wrong, and dangerous ways to be, they could show me my Inner Team's rules of the right, virtuous and safe ways to be:

- I should be hard working and productive, and not stop until the work is done.
- I should speak or write only when I have no gaps in my knowledge.
- I should express myself with errorless clarity (preferably in one draft).

This led naturally to the next question: "Whose rules are these?"

These rules came from three characters on my Inner Team:

- The rule about working hard comes from the **Pusher.**
- The rule about being completely expert comes from the **Expert.**
- The rule about perfect clarity comes from the **Perfectionist.**

Knowing that all characters have protective intentions allowed me to reinterpret their actions as attempts to protect rather than sabotage me. Here's what I discovered:

Pusher operates by the rule that whatever your problem, taking action is the answer, offering the advice that discipline, focus and determined hard work were the key to getting the book finished. It was trying to produce energy and drive to get me through the hard slog of writing. It wanted to keep me on track to my goal by taking action rather than wasting energy on rumination and self-doubt. It was trying to protect me by steering me away from the risks associated with overthinking and failing to take action.

Expert operates by the rule that safety comes from having the answers. For the Expert, ignorance is unforgivably dangerous. It was trying to protect me from this by ensuring that I was rigorous in my thinking about the ideas I included in the book, and that I hadn't left out crucial information. It advised me to study a lot more, perhaps earn a PhD in the topic, gather more evidence and question every assumption before even *contemplating* publishing my ideas.

Perfectionist operates by the rule that errors and faults are dangerous, so everything can and should be improved. It was trying to protect me by ensuring this would be the very best book I could write. It was protecting me from feeling regret about muddled writing which could have been prevented with a little extra diligence and discernment. It was trying to steer me away from the risks associated with carelessness, and advised an extra round (or ten) of edits before publication.

By naming and turning towards these characters to acknowledge their protective role, my tangled mess of confused thoughts had sorted itself out into three distinctive points of view, each amplified by the Inner Critic until it got my attention. What had felt like an attack by three dangerous saboteurs began to feel more like supportive advice from concerned friends.

THE TENACIOUS DEFENDERS

I wish I could say that this shift in perspective immediately lifted me out of my creative funk. It gave me more understanding and self-compassion, yes, but I couldn't seem to restore that elusive sense of flow to my writing.

Whenever I decided to take a break, my Pusher would tell me that if I stopped now, I might never restart.

I'd start writing about a character, and my Expert would ask me "Are you sure? What if you're wrong?". I'd find myself reading articles, following references, ordering books, talking to friends to learn everything I could. A morning reserved for writing often turned into a close examination of an obscure research rabbit hole.

When I would finally get a messy first draft of a chapter onto the page, my Perfectionist would implore me to edit it right away, because it was simply not acceptable to leave it in this condition. It felt like the grammar police were banging on the proverbial door, sharpened red pencils in hand.

Each character was protective, but each had a narrow and incomplete set of solutions. Pusher could get me into action but didn't permit me to slow down or rest. Expert prompted me to study and read but couldn't identify when I knew enough. Perfectionist set a high standard for quality, but couldn't see what was good enough, especially for a first draft.

I was stuck in a vicious cycle. The more these characters nagged me, the more pressure I would put on myself to write perfect sentences, to critically evaluate my ideas, to achieve ever more demanding words-per-day targets.

Unsurprisingly, doubling down on the same strategies didn't produce a different result. I missed deadline after deadline. The quality of what I was producing seemed to me to be pretty terrible. What had begun as a delightful creative flow had become a turgid grind. The completion of the book felt like a mountain I could not possibly climb.

So, I stopped writing. I walked away.

My Critic immediately reversed course, and told me that was a fatal mistake, and also proof positive that I really was too lazy and undisciplined to finish the book. When I would even *contemplate* restarting my writing, my Critic would remind me that my writing was crap, my thinking a sloppy mess full of holes. I was damned if I did, damned if I didn't.

LEANING INTO THE FEAR

A month into my two-week break (euphemistically labeled my "creative pause") I wrote this question in my journal: *What am I afraid of?*

For once, the writing flowed, and it boiled down to one terrifying truth: finishing the book would prove, once and for all, that I actually <u>was</u> lazy, ignorant, and sloppy.

Terrified that this might be the truth of me, I had poured all my energy into proving that it was not.

How was I trying to prove that I wasn't lazy? By working hard. Unceasingly.

That I wasn't ignorant? By studying and researching. Endlessly.

That I wasn't sloppy? By editing and rewriting. Constantly.

My effort to disprove what I feared might be true about me did <u>not</u> have the desired effect of erasing my fear. I'd forgotten one of the principles of working with the Inner Critic: don't try and please or appease it, because nothing you do will ever be enough. The Critic exists to criticize. That's its job. It's not going to magically become a champion and cheerleader, telling you *"You've worked hard enough, what you wrote today was terrific, why not put your slippers on and take a well-earned break?"*

TURNING TOWARD THE FEAR

If I couldn't <u>prove</u> that I wasn't lazy, ignorant, and sloppy, I wouldn't play that game. What if I stopped trying to defend myself against these accusations?

What I saw is that these descriptions <u>are</u> true of me, some of the time.

- I am lazy and undisciplined sometimes. I am also hard-working.

- I am ignorant and have many gaps in my knowledge. I also have a lot of experience and expertise.

- I can be careless and sloppy, and I can also be careful and diligent.

The more I noticed and named these paradoxes within me, the more the fear dissipated. What did these supposed defects and flaws prove, after all? That I'm imperfect. Inconsistent. Human.

With no further need to defend myself from these accusations, someone could have yelled in my face that I was a lazy, talentless hack, and I would have smiled and agreed that yes, sometimes I was.

Faced with proof of my messy humanness rather than my irredeemable worthlessness, what began to emerge was self-compassion and a long-overdue restoration of my sense of humor. I could own my laziness, my ignorance, and my error-filled work, and laugh at them.

FROM JUDGMENT TO CURIOSITY

As my self-judgments dissipated and my defenses dropped away, something else emerged in their place: curiosity.

No longer afraid to admit it was there, I started to get curious about the lazy part of me. I discovered that it's not really lazy, it simply doesn't have anywhere it needs to get in a hurry. It likes to pause, daydream, take naps, to let inspiration find me.

As I connected with this part of myself, my relationship with time started to shift. The pressure to get back to work receded, and as it faded, so too did the familiar tension in my neck and shoulders. In the place of that tension was not only bodily relaxation, but a gentle, unfocused attention to the moment, to what could be seen, heard, felt, experienced right here and right now.

I was experiencing a character on my Inner Team called Being, the opposite of the Pusher. It was the Pusher who pejoratively labeled him "Lazy". When I would take breaks, my Pusher would quickly remind me that I was falling behind the word target for the day. But when I checked in with Being, he reminded me that when I was rested and present, the writing would flow. And he was right, most of the time.

Now when I got stuck or lost the plot, I would take a break, shift my focus to the present moment, enjoy whatever my eyes rested on, and let my body move in whatever ways it wanted to. More often than not, I would return to my writing with my sense of flow re-established. The anxiety and urgency that accompanied my Pusher did not disappear, but its intensity was significantly decreased. I relaxed into my word targets, rather than slogging my exhausted way towards them. In Being, I had discovered a resource I desperately needed, not just to complete the book, but to experience joy in the process of writing.

Much as I enjoyed the newly rediscovered flow that Being generated, I still needed my Pusher. The work of writing a book still required effort, discipline, and a dose of determination. I needed both. When my Pusher would offer its familiar refrain that I might never return if I took a break, I'd mentally check in with Being, who always seemed to have the right answer: rest is part of action. Look at athletes: if they didn't include rest days, their performance would decline, and injury would be inevitable.

I would work for a while, and then when I started to tire, I would rest. When I felt rested, I would want to return to writing, and didn't need the crack of the Pusher's verbal whip to get me back to my desk. I no longer needed my daily word targets to motivate me. I surfed the waves of activity and rest, activity and rest. Some days produced more or better writing than others, but I was making progress again. My battered confidence began, word by word, to heal.

My curiosity now led me to extend this exploration. If this is what was possible by turning towards my lazy part, what might happen if I turned towards the parts of me that I'd labeled ignorant and sloppy?

My fear of being ignorant came from my Expert. Its opposite was a character called **Learner**. As I got to know this part through journaling, I found a gentler, more forgiving way of navigating the uncertainties of thinking and writing. The Learner reminded me that knowing everything about the topic was not a necessary prerequisite to sharing ideas. Knowledge is always incomplete and will always evolve. The more you know, the more you realize what you don't know. Every answer begs more questions. Focus on what you're learning rather than what you don't know yet.

My fear of being sloppy came from my Perfectionist. Its opposite was **Messy**, a character who embraces all forms of mess, including mental mess (confusion), emotional mess (ambivalence) to spiritual mess (purposelessness). Messy's message to me was to embrace it all. Perfect order isn't a requirement for the book to be useful. It's the humanness and incompleteness that makes it relatable. Messy reassured me that every first draft of every book ever written was (you guessed it) a mess. This was something to embrace rather than hide: the freedom to make a mess is rocket fuel for creativity (as any kid with fingerpaints knows).

With Pusher's driven intensity balanced by the unhurried flow of Being, I learned to renew my energy, to not deplete myself by overworking.

With Expert's demand for intellectual certainty balanced by Learner's endless, questioning curiosity and excitement about new insights, I found confidence to share what I did know, without worrying about what I didn't.

With Perfectionist's exacting standards balanced by Messy's experimental permissiveness, I was able to shift from performing to exploring. The goal was no longer meeting a standard of perfection but allowing myself to experiment. Now I could embrace that mapping the maze required both finding the dead ends *and* the promising avenues and realizing that I couldn't know ahead of time which was which.

WHAT I LEARNED ABOUT MY INNER TEAM

My Inner Team was both the cause of my stuckness, and its solution. My Pusher, Expert and Perfectionist were each necessary but insufficient. The larger, more diverse Inner Team of Pusher and Being, Expert and Learner, Perfectionist and Messy, provided me the resources I needed to complete the task.

The insight that opened the possibility of their reintegration was, in retrospect, a blinding flash of the obvious. It wasn't me judging Being as lazy, Learner as ignorant, or Messy as sloppy. It was Pusher, Expert and Perfectionist who were judging and labeling their respective opposites. And I didn't have to agree with them.

What enabled me to separate from the points of view of each of these three powerful characters was the continuing emergence of my Inner Leader. This enabled me to observe the thoughts, feelings, beliefs, and fears of each character, without agreeing with them. Each character held a partial truth, worth hearing and exploring. But no single character could get me to my goal on its own. Pusher had the strength to get me into action but didn't know how to slow down or rest. Expert prompted me to study and read but couldn't identify when I knew enough. Perfectionist set a high standard for quality, but couldn't see what was good enough, especially for a first draft.

As I accessed my Inner Leader, what arose within me was curiosity, compassion and humor. My former judgment, fear and anxiety didn't disappear, but they no longer stopped me taking action toward my goal. The Critic's attacks became less frequent, less fierce, and easier to shake off.

And the blank screen filled with words.

GLOSSARY OF INNER TEAM DIALOGUE TERMS

Character

A consistent and identifiable pattern of thoughts, feelings, sensations and beliefs, manifesting as a set of rules for behavior. Also known as parts, subpersonalities, selves and voices.

Insider Character

A Character on your Inner Team who is a primary protector of your safety, and the source of some of your most reliable strengths. Insiders are typically the loudest, most active and most easily recognized characters on your Inner Team. Together, your Insiders form your identity, your persona, and who you think you are.

Operating Committee

A group of Insider characters who cooperate, support and reinforce each other to protect you. This is the "in crowd" of your Inner Team, who hold onto power to direct your thinking and actions, and guard against the influence of Outsiders. The Operating Committee is indistinguishable from what you describe as your personality. Typically comprised of 3-5 Insiders.

Outsider Character
A character on your Inner who has been ignored, rejected, marginalized or even forgotten altogether (disowned). They're the voices on your Inner Team that have been shouted down, silenced or suppressed, because they are perceived to be a threat to your Insiders' approach to keep you safe. Outsiders are hard to see in yourself and are often projected onto other people.

Inner Team
A metaphor to describe the interaction of all characters who represent an aspect of who you are, both Insiders and Outsiders. Typically experienced as "the committee in your head".

Inner Leader
Who you really are, when you strip away the patterns of thinking, feeling and behavior described by your characters. The Inner Leader is not a character, but a process and a practice of being conscious of your characters. An observing, witnessing presence that can recognize, appreciate and coordinate the actions of all characters on your Inner Team.

Opposite Characters
Two characters that have opposite, directly contrasting beliefs, behaviors and ways of being in the world. Opposite characters operate as polarities, describing principles that seem contradictory but are actually interdependent. You cannot choose one

side of a polarity over its opposite and expect to thrive over time. They are balances to find, not problems to solve.

Integration
The process of becoming more whole. Typically involves managing the over-contribution of Insiders, and re-admitting Outsiders back into the Inner Team.

APPENDIX B

ORIGINS OF
INNER TEAM DIALOGUE

Inner Team Dialogue is based on Voice Dialogue and the Psychology of Selves, a parts-work framework and method that was created by two brilliant PhD psychologists, Drs Hal and Sidra Stone, beginning in the 1970's. The inclusion of the word "Dialogue" in the name 'Inner Team Dialogue' is a direct nod of recognition to the influence of the Stones' extraordinary work.

ITD shares some core principles found in Internal Family Systems, including the premise that there are no bad parts, a non-pathologizing approach to protective parts, and the centrality of the Inner Leader (Self) as the source of healing and change.

For readers who are familiar with IFS and/or Voice Dialogue, here's a quick terminology comparison.

INNER TEAM DIALOGUE	VOICE DIALOGUE	INTERNAL FAMILY SYSTEMS
Inner Leader	Aware Ego Process	Self
Characters	Selves	Parts
Insiders	Primary Selves	Managers, Firefighters and Protectors
Outsiders	Disowned Selves	Exiles

How ITD Differs from Voice Dialogue

ITD aims to remain true to the spirit of Voice Dialogue, but because it emerged from the practice of coaching rather than psychotherapy, it diverges in a few notable ways.

Terminology: ITD uses terminology which is designed to be accessible for a wide range of clients who might seek coaching. The Inner Team metaphor is used to make the inherent abstractness of parts work more understandable. ITD minimizes the use of clinical and psychological terminology, for example replacing "Aware Ego Process" with the term "Inner Leader".

Polarities: The Stones explored the idea of opposite selves and the importance of their integration but did not explore their relationship as polarities. This polarity perspective is central to ITD and illuminates many of the inner dynamics that occur within the Inner Team.

Coaching Frame: Voice Dialogue and IFS were both developed by therapists, for use in therapeutic practice. Inner Team Dialogue was developed by a coach, to fit within a coach's non-clinical scope of practice, and to meet the needs of coaching clients.

CONTINUING YOUR
INNER TEAM JOURNEY

Learning more about Inner Team Dialogue

This book is intended to provide a resource for coaches, coaching clients and serious seekers on their journey to a more integrated, whole experience of being alive. It's our hope that you will have found the information in this book useful, perhaps even illuminating.

If you're a coach or therapist:

Inner Team Dialogue practitioner training is available to those with formal training in coaching or psychotherapy/counseling. For details of upcoming courses, check out the Trainings page at www.innerteamdialogue.com

If you'd like to find an ITD qualified coach:

Many people are introduced to Inner Team Dialogue by their coach. If you've found your way here by other means and would like to experience this approach firsthand, please email info@innerteamdialogue.com to request a referral of a qualified practitioner.

For other questions:

Send an email to info@innerteamdialogue.com, or use the form found at https://www.innerteamdialogue.com/contact and we'll do our best to respond timely.

BIBLIOGRAPHY

Barrett, L. F. (2020). *How emotions are made: The secret life of the brain.* PICADOR.

Brown, B. (2021). *Atlas of the heart.* Random House UK.

Brown, B. (2020). *The gifts of Imperfection / Brene Brown.* Random House.

Brown, B. (2019). *Braving the wilderness: The quest for true belonging and the courage to stand alone.* Random House.

Dyak, M. (1999). *The Voice Dialogue Facilitators Handbook.* L-I-F-E Energy Press.

Earley, J., & Schwartz, R. C. (2022). *Self-therapy: A step-by-step guide to creating wholeness using IFS, a cutting-edge psychotherapy.* Pattern Systems Books.

Emerson, B., & Lewis, K. (2019). *Navigating polarities: Using both/and thinking to lead transformation.* Paradoxical Press.

Erickson, V. (2015). *Edge of wonder.* Enrealment Press.

Germer, C. K., & Siegel, R. D. (2012). *Wisdom and compassion in psychotherapy: Deepening mindfulness in clinical practice.* Guilford Press.

Hoffman, D. (2012). *The Voice Dialogue Anthology: Explorations of the Psychology of selves and the aware ego process*. Delos, Inc.

Holmes, T., Holmes, L., & Eckstein, S. (2007). *Parts work: An illustrated guide to your inner life*. Winged Heart Press.

Johnson, B. A. (2014). *Polarity Management identifying and managing unsolvable problems*. HRD Press.

Kegan, R., & Lahey, L. L. (2009). *Immunity to change: How to overcome it and unlock the potential in yourself and your organization*. Harvard Business Review Press.

Miller, William (2021). *On Second Thought: How Ambivalence Shapes Your Life*. Guildford Press.

Moore M. *Coaching the Multiplicity of Mind: A Strengths-based Model*. Glob Adv Health Med. 2013 Jul;2(4):78-84. doi: 10.7453/gahmj.2013.030. PMID: 24416685; PMCID: PMC3833551.

Niedra, Astra (2019): *Which Self are you? An Overview of Inner Selves, with an Introduction to Voice Dialogue* (PDF publication, retrieved from https://www.voicedialogue.com/which-self-are-you/)

Pangaia, J. ona. (2012). *An Introduction to Voice Dialogue: Finding the benefit of people who bug you*. Heart of the Garden Publishing.

Pressfield, S. (2012). *Turning pro: Tap your inner power and create your life's work*. Mallory International Ltd.

Rowan, J. (2017). *Discover your subpersonalities: Our inner world and the people in it*. Routledge.

Schwartz, R. C. (2017). *Many minds, one self: Evidence for a radical shift in paradigm*. Trailhead Publications.

Schwartz, R. C. (2023). *No bad parts: Healing trauma & restoring wholeness*. Vermilion.

Stone, H., & Stone, S. (1997). *Embracing Our Selves: The Voice Dialogue manual*. Nataraj Publishing.

Stone, H., & Stone, S. (2011). *Embracing your inner critic: Turning self-criticism into a creative asset*. Harper.

Stone, H., & Stone, S. (2000). *Partnering: A new kind of relationship*. New World Library.

Stone, H., Stone, S., & Stone, H. (1989). *Embracing each other: Relationship as teacher, Healer & Guide*. Nataraj Pub.

V. der Kolk. B. (2015). *The body keeps the score: Mind, brain and body in the transformation of trauma*. Penguin Books.

Video:

Harris, Dan (2022). *The Benefits of Not Being a Jerk to Yourself*, Ted Talk, https://www.youtube.com/watch?v=NuhIzO57HVk&ab_channel=TED

Longdon, Eleanor (2013). *The Voices in My Head*, Ted Talk https://www.youtube.com/watch?v=syjEN3peC-Jw&list=RDLVe6Rvae1IBms&index=26&ab_channel=TED

Fernyhough, Charles (2016): *The Science of the Voices in Your Head*, The Royal Institution, https://www.youtube.com/watch?v=95ot-BlepVHc&t=1299s&ab_channel=TheRoyalInstitution

ABOUT THE AUTHOR

 **Paul Wyman, PCC, CPPC** is an experienced professional coach, with over 25 years of experience. He has coached individuals from all walks of life, specializing in leadership and executive coaching. He has served in a range of roles in the Leadership Development field, from leading an Organization Development team in an academic medical center to serving as an internal executive coach for a major global organization. Throughout his career he has been involved in coach development, qualifying as a coaching supervisor in 2017.

Paul's coaching has prominently featured parts-work methods to support his clients' self-awareness, self-compassion and capacity to lead consciously. In 2020, at the prompting of several clients who'd experienced the power of this approach, he founded Inner Team Dialogue, to make the method available to coaches and their clients. Hundreds of professional coaches now use this transformational method in their own lives, and with their clients, with remarkable results. Using plain language and relatable stories, Paul has simplified the challenge of making sense of your inner world and has become a sought-after facilitator and teacher. Inner Team Dialogue has emerged as a uniquely powerful method for coaches, particularly those practicing in the leadership and vertical development space.

Paul is an honors graduate of the University of York, and studied at Vassar College. He received his coaching certification in 1998 through the Coaches Training Institute, and his Diploma in Coaching Supervision through the Coaching Supervision Academy in 2017. He has held the Professional Certified Coach designation since 2015.

Originally from England, Paul has lived in the US since 1991, and in Colorado since 1995. When not coaching, Paul can be found playing in online Scrabble tournaments (which means he can spell many more words than he can define) and riding his bike (very slowly) up Colorado's mountains. He's mildly obsessed with octopuses. He lives near Boulder with his wife, Anne, and two rambunctious cats.

INDEX

Adventurer, see Thrill Seeker

Allower, 91

Artist, 55

Being, 175

Boundaried, 160

Challenger, see Warrior

Chameleon, 61

Character, 16

Collaborator, 76

Comfort Seeker, 67

Competitor, 73

Confident, see Expert

Consultation, 265

Controller, 87

Decision making, 257-275

Dependent, 97

Disowned Selves, See Outsider

Dissociative Identity Disorder, 7

Expert, 79

Feeling, 182

Free Agent, 119

Hidden Insider, 23

Humble, see Learner

Hypochondriac, 228

Improviser, 154

Inclusiveness, 289

Independent, 94

Indulger, 101

Inner Critic, 231-240

Inner Leader, 21, 245-255

Inner Parenting, 226

Inner Team, 20, 41

Insider, 22

Internal Family Systems, 7, 8, 248, 252, 311

Journaling, 277-287

Judge, 107

Leadership Vacuum, 22

Learner, 82

Loyalist, 117

Material, 122

Matriarch, 143

Maximizer, 131

Mercenary, See Free Agent
Messy, 148
Minimizer, 129
Monomind, 8,9
Multiple Mind, 3, 10-13, 258

Naming, 49
Neutral, 113

Observer, 137
Operating Committee, 26
Optimist, See Trusting
Ordinary, 202, 30-33
Outsider, 26-30

Participant, 135
Parts, see Character
Patriarch, 141
Peacemaker, 208
Perfectionist, 145
Pessimist, See Protector
Planner, 151
Playful, 189
Pleaser, 157
Polarities, 38
Pragmatist, 57
Primary Selves, see Insiders
Princess, See Special
Protector, 164
Pusher, 172

Rational, 179
Rebel, 196
Responsible, 186
Restrictor, 103

Rule Breaker, see Rebel
Rule Follower, 192

Saver, see Restrictor
Schema, 19-20
Self (IFS), See Inner Leader
Selves (Voice Dialogue), see
    Character
Special, 199, 30-33
Spender, see Indulger
Spiritual, 125

Thrill Seeker, 70
Trauma, 7, 20, 167, 217, 219,
    227
Trusting, 168

Victim, 228
Voice Dialogue, 47, 311, 312
Vulnerable Child, 42, 213-229

Warrior, 206
Whiplash, 271-275

Zebra, 63